Seventy and Speaking Up

An Anthology of Essays Written by Women in their Seventies Sharing their Truths, Triumphs and Transitions

Edited by Georgina O'Hara Callan

Print ISBN 979-8-9989714-2-6

Ebook ISBN 979-8-9989714-3-3

Contents

Dedication

This book is dedicated to all the women who have bravely spoken up about aging, helping to shift the narrative away from stereotypical wrinkles and anticipated decrepitude towards vibrancy, lifelong learning, enthusiasm for life itself, and the opportunities within, as well as acceptance. While we are not ageless—we all have a birthdate—we can choose how we age as we chose how to live.

Jenna

"Do less, not more, with the time that's still available to you. But do less with more intention, with more thought and preparation, and with more care.

Do less, but do it with love. Say 'no' more often, and say 'yes' to what really matters to you. My goal is to leave the regrets in my life as just that, regrets, tidied away in a box I no longer need to open, and proceed into my seventies with wisdom, grace, and a passion for life.

I don't regret who I was, how I once looked—well, maybe a little—but what do I expect? To look the same forever? One thing I am determined to do is not to be preoccupied or disappointed by my appearance. What is the point? Could someone tell me the point of that?

I've realized that if I'm happy with my 'inner' self, then I am less concerned with my 'outer' appearance."

Acknowledgement

One never writes a book alone. There are, of course, the amazing women who contributed to this book anonymously or otherwise, without whom the book could never have been written.

However the essayists decided to write—some eager, some less so—I am grateful that they wanted to read their thoughts and words in print, and that they shared with me the idea that the more we speak up, the more other women will be encouraged to do the same thing and speak up and speak out about their lives.

To all the essayists, I would like to extend a heartfelt thank you. It is gratifying to me that so many of you told me how you "enjoyed the process." Because writing is a process, once the essays had been written, they had to be edited for comprehension, grammar, spelling, and context, and ultimately follow the procedural rules of chapters and fitting words to a page without losing any context, meaning, or intent. I appreciate your patience with the process.

Speaking Up is the best thing we can do for ourselves and for each other, and for the women of the future.

To everyone who has been involved in *Seventy and Speaking Up*, I sincerely thank you.

Introduction

Time is more valuable when there is less of it

F or many women, seventy is just another number, inevitable (if you're lucky) but nothing special. For other women, the number seventy looms large, representing a landmark: the first step, perhaps, into a world where there exists a sense of finality.

It wasn't that long ago that women in their sixties and seventies were described as "elderly," a word that may create an image of a bent, frail, gray-haired women, who may also have been depicted as being alone. For many women today, that image is completely unrelatable. Women are leading extraordinary lives in their sixties, seventies, eighties, and even into their nineties.

It's not just that we take better care of ourselves than in previous generations, understanding that a sedentary life before and after retirement is a health risk. We know more about our bodies and how they function, and we are open to understanding our inner selves; we seek help when we need it, and, most significantly, we live by our own rules and expectations, not those of others.

We aren't the only ones. In books and articles, there are stories of women who became legends, women who reached beyond the expectations of their time, pioneering women in medicine, technology, and just about every field in which men also succeeded.

But so often, these women in the past were viewed as anomalies, as exceptions, while simultaneously being lauded and praised; meanwhile, the majority of women continued with more traditional roles—and expected lives—for generations.

The focus has shifted. Today, we read about the lives of actresses and musicians who are still working into their seventies and sometimes their eighties, filling concert venues and theaters. The more that older women are seen as viable, the more opportunities there will be for older women to be less marginalized in society and lead lives that earlier generations could never have imagined: active, vibrant, and intentional lives. Lives that are increasingly led out of the shadows, with women demonstrating that old age is no longer a quiet place to occupy, out of everyone else's way, in solitude and possible isolation.

But what of women who aren't famous? We don't have to be famous to make an impression, to make a difference, whether that's a quiet impression or a loud one. Women have always been open to sharing and learning from each other, and in many cases social media has provided the platform to do this. We have a unique opportunity today to be more connected than ever before, to learn more about each other, and, in doing so, to encourage one another to pursue all the dreams we may have shelved in earlier decades.

This book is about women who are navigating the decade of the seventies. If the sixties are the decade of "do what you can while you can" what words should we adopt, and live by for the decade of the seventies?

As I write the introduction to this book, I am about six months away from turning seventy. "What," you may well ask, "does someone know about being in one's seventies—enough to write a book—if you haven't experienced the decade?"

Unlike turning sixty, a decade that I cruised into as an extension of my fifties, feeling that I would address being in my sixties one day, at some later date, I have given being in my seventies a lot of thought. For me, turning the chapter on page sixty-nine and opening the chapter on becoming seventy is a very different feeling than sliding from fifty-nine to sixty.

Only vestiges remain of who I once was in my early sixties, while my fifties are becoming a distant memory by the month. Who do I want to be in my seventies? It is actually a choice....but we often don't realize that. It is a choice because many of us have the one thing that makes choice possible, and that is opportunity. In this case, the opportunity to choose who we want to be in our seventies.

My comfort in writing about the decade of the seventies is due in large part to the writing and editing of *Sixty and Speaking Up,* a book that showcased the voices of women in their sixties who were willing to speak up about their personal experiences of the decade. Reflection, introspection, and addressing thoughts and fears about the future are inherent in any narration of individual experience.

Between these two books, *Sixty and Speaking Up* and *Seventy and Speaking Up,* I have spent a great deal of time researching the decades. I have spoken to many women and listened to their stories, their hopes and concerns, and, most importantly, their personal comprehension of these decades—a far different experience than that of our mothers and grandmothers.

We all understand that today, time is in shorter supply than it was a decade ago, and I want to be prepared. I want the remaining years of my life—ten or twenty years, although I'll settle for around fifteen years—to be important in a way I am still defining. But the point is that I am consciously defining how I want to live my life, rather than just ambling along—although if it suits you, ambling is fine.

A quick glance at the statistics of heavily assisted old age—from care homes, to daily in-home nursing and domestic help, physical ailments, and the fear of cognitive decline—encourages me to make the most of my time here.

And maybe I want to throw caution to the wind in the process—but that's a story for later in the book.

Who do I want to be in my seventies? What attributes do I want to share about myself, to modify, to adjust and why am I even thinking this way?

While I understand that I want to be "ageless," I also recognize that this is an impossibility. We cannot be "ageless" because we all have a birthdate that defines our age—our start date. We are tied to a date we're unable to alter.

We can, however, be "ageless" in attitude, even if it means working harder to understand the rapidly changing world about us, retaining an open mind to things not being the way we once understood them, and maintaining age positivity by remaining active and engaged, and, frankly, wearing what we want, and saying and doing what we want without fear of censure.

Nothing ages us more than being befuddled by technology or confused in trying to understand that social rules, once guideposts for us, continue to change, along with values and traditions. The shape of life itself is changing around us, as we will remember from when we were young, hearing from our parents and grandparents about how their world had changed.

"Things just aren't like they used to be" was the most often-heard refrain. What they were expressing was the idea that if only we could go back in time to when the world made sense—although did it ever make sense?—they would feel better about life.

And now we're here. As with *Sixty and Speaking Up*, I've spoken to many women in their sixties and seventies, as well as a number who are in their eighties.

I've met intractable "grandmas" rooted in their views, loudly disapproving: "I don't agree with that," applying those words to everything, anything, and everyone.

I've talked to women who blithely say they "don't understand what all the fuss is about: we all have to age" and to women who have revved up their lives in their seventies, sometimes to compensate for the lack of activity during their sixties—maybe it took part of a decade to find the courage—and sometimes because they are naturally confident and adventurous, or perhaps they are embarking on the decade with the overriding sense that time is short and their health is not improving.

There are precautionary tales often precipitated by a health crisis followed by promises to take better care. There is loss, whether expected or unexpected, that changes the immediate lives of many, while others look on, sympathetic, but all that's really said at the time is, "It's the age, you know; we should expect this."

For myself, I was curious about the decade of the seventies, not least because I felt that the shocks, trials, triumphs, and transitions I'd experienced in my sixties would subside in my seventies. In large part, this was because I had come to terms with the preparation the sixties decade creates, and that is the confrontation of mortality.

This opportunity often arises due to the ever-diminishing responsibilities and demands on our time. We may have more, not less, time, to think and act, while there is less time overall.

Although the seventies may present opportunities for one last chance to take an adventure—if one is inclined—it's not all over, there are more than a few women who are still taking large and small leaps in life in their eighties, and they are much to be admired.

Peggy

"It isn't our age that defines us, it's our attitude. Our attitude to life, and to others, overshadows how we look. I believe people react and respond to other people, regardless of how they look. Once they start talking, communicating, with each other, their outward appearances are meaningless. If you like someone, you don't care how they look, you only care about how they think.

Friends are lifelines. Old friends, new friends, acquaintances, casual friends, everyone is someone important if you can find common ground. Of the billions of people in the world, we may find ourselves, if we're lucky, with a handful of people around us. Treasure these people and don't push them aside. They are the people who will carry your memory."

Chapter One

Meet the writers

The women who spoke up

It takes courage to write about your thoughts and feelings, especially when you know others will read your words and, inevitably, form opinions.

How did women learn about this project? As with *Sixty and Speaking Up* there was a sense of serendipity about editing this anthology.

On a Facebook page, women posted, "Why not a book about women in their seventies? I have something to say." Other women reached out through my website, which I'd shared with writers and author groups.

Several writers approached me as a result of the efforts of the essayists in *Sixty and Speaking Up*. And yet other writers were women I'd known throughout my life whose paths had taken different directions—women I hadn't spoken to in decades. However, we were loosely aware of one another via social media.

In short, there were connections, women who knew women, with only a tiny percentage being women I knew before writing my previous book. It's a beautiful thing when strangers unite in a common effort.

I have been fortunate to meet some amazing women, for both books, *Sixty and Speaking Up* and *Seventy and Speaking Up,* and you will have the opportunity to meet the women of the latter title in these pages.

Although I didn't know exactly what to expect from the essayists, I did have expectations, because if you wish to speak out, I think you are likely to have something to say that will encourage other women to speak up and share their lives and experiences.

The framework for the book and the essays was to avoid topics that can divide more than unite us (religion and politics, for example) and to focus instead on the experience of being in one's seventies, because there is so much to say about this decade.

Predictably, at this age, there is something of a chronological reckoning, a recounting of a life so far, but the mission for the essayists was to think about women of a similar age who would be reading and relating to the words. Some women asked specifically if they could write about health or sex, while others just wanted to think about things for a while before submitting their essays.

There are many themes that women have elected to write about in this book. Health and relationships are the two most prominent, but there are so many others as lives are contemplated: lives lived, loves, both lost and found, goals, and accomplishments.

Some essays reflect on the distant past while bringing us up to date with current events, while others focus on the present and the future. Women wrote about what they are doing now and what they plan to do next. Honesty prevails throughout the book, with disappointments shared alongside unexpected shifts in life, triumphs, revelations, and plans to move forwards. There is also a celebration of accomplishments—many unexpected and unplanned—as well as the narration of the joy in the discovery of new things and in new exploration.

In a similar way to *Sixty and Speaking Up,* this book has two types of contributors. There are women, including a few professional writers, who are identified by their name and state, county, or province, depending on whether they live in the USA, UK, or Canada, who wished to write their own words and they have written chapter-length essays.

Another group of women wished to write about their thoughts on being in their seventies as a paragraph or two, and these excerpts appear between chapters. They are designed to insert thoughts, ideas, and observations, into longer pieces of writing.

Many women wanted to be anonymous for reasons I respect, and, in these cases, whether they chose to write a chapter or an anecdote, they are identified by a first name only, which may have been changed.

Whatever topics the writers chose—whether finding or losing love, the changing dynamics of relationships with family and friends, work, creativity, health, continuity, abrupt changes, or any of the other events and experiences in life—there is one thing everyone has in common. Every writer has given considerable thought to the meaning of this decade, and to do that, they have reflected on their lives.

I am grateful to everyone who has been—who was—willing to be introspective, for to write about the past and meld it to the present under a banner of being in one's seventies requires considerable introspection, alongside a willingness to look backward, and forward, at the same time, and to confront the decisions we've made and the paths we've chosen for reasons we may no longer recognize.

In looking backward we must be willing to affirm that we did the best we could—or that perhaps we could have done better—to accept the accountability therein, and to acknowledge regrets alongside highlighting the many pleasurable memories.

Several essayists have described this process as "life-affirming" and experienced validation of their lives by writing down their observations. I found this sentiment to be heartwarming, driving me forward to complete the book.

I hope that you will find these honest, heartfelt, warm, and inspirational essays and words encouraging and that they will inspire you and other women to speak up about aging and being in one's seventies. When women encourage each other it is always a win.

Catherine

"To be honest, I am glad my sixties are over and I am in my seventies. It feels as if I have a clean slate to start over with a new decade. Although I'm a little less mobile and I have a few more wrinkles, I've lost a great deal of anxiety about aging in general. It is very liberating."

Sharon

"I know women who have made it their mission to live as long as possible. These determined, sometimes defiant, women, who are happy to shout about how long they plan to live to anyone willing to listen, can be intimidating. Longevity is their main goal in life, to defeat the odds, upend the statistics, as if in reaching their nineties and beyond, they will win the battle. Do they believe the reward is to cheat mortality?

Who are they trying to convince? Even the fittest, most vibrant women age. It's a question of *how* one lives, not stating timelines and goals for *how long* one lives. Isn't that missing the point about life? While the intention to live a long healthy life is a good one, why carry out this intention in such an oppositional manner?

I think these pronouncements are about fear, and are often stated by those who have yet to resolve their own sense of mortality. Some women may carry many regrets about their lives, and I think they are really saying, 'It wasn't the best life, and I didn't get everything I wanted, but at least it was a long life.'"

Chapter Two

Judy Devlin

Love, life, and letting go

After seven decades of living, Judy believes that everything she's experienced so far has prepared her for this stage of her life. All the ups and downs have given her knowledge, experience, and the wisdom to value herself and choose wisely how she spends the last part of her life.

"It has always felt to me that I had an abundance of love in my life. I have memories of feeling a deep love for my parents, my sister, and many family members, and, especially during my childhood, memories of my maternal aunts. I'm sure I confused lust with love in my early twenties, but perhaps all in preparation to love more deeply as I've aged.

The sweet joy of aging has been feeling genuine love for myself, without much judgment, and accepting my shortcomings. It allows me to minimize past failures and maximize pleasant memories. It has put me on a path towards loving others and expressing that love freely throughout my life.

Deciding to became a nurse in college and then pursing a career as a nurse practitioner shaped my life. It led me to a variety of career opportunities I could never have imagined. In 1978, I drove from Richmond, Virginia, to San Francisco to pursue my master's degree, which ultimately led to a nurse practitioner certification. I'll never forget the thrill of independence driving into the state of California, where I'd never been before, and traveling up the beautiful coastal highway.

Equipped with the necessary certification, I made a significant change twenty-five years ago to oncology. I stretched to learn the rich science of cancer, the human experience, and how to navigate its complexities for patients and families. At times, I felt I learned more from patients and families than they did from me. Watching patients face significant illness and mortality with grace and dignity gave me a roadmap for myself. It's telling that, while I am retired, I stay involved with an advisory council because leaving it all behind felt incomplete.

Equally important to my career choice was the man I married forty-five years ago. Our friendship and love have deepened over the years, and I believe we've both been good for one another. I cannot imagine life without him, and I hope that if that is my destiny, I will cope and find a way to live well.

What I once valued is now less important than my relationships and making a difference in the lives of the family and friends I love so dearly. In my earlier decades, it was important to do as much as I could each day, often at the expense of unnecessary stress. I had several lists to keep all the balls juggling. I valued being organized, on time, and indispensable at home and at work.

Eventually, it caught up with me, and I found some short-term therapy to help me sort out my stress and gain practical strategies to live better. I feel that this new decade might even help me reach a place where I can embrace those strategies.

There's no doubt that becoming a grandmother has been one of the most incredible gifts of aging. Our four grandsons fill me with emotional joy and leave me feeling like my life's newest purpose is to love and nurture them. It's a deep and recurring joy! There's such relief in not feeling that heavy responsibility for their outcomes, just a hope to influence their little lives positively.

I carry a quote in my wallet that I read around a decade ago and it reminds me to focus on what truly matters: 'In the end, only three things matter: how much you loved, how gently you lived, and how gracefully you let go of things not meant for you.' (*Buddha's Little Instruction Book* by Jack Kornfield)."

Judy Devlin, Texas, USA.

"I don't think the seventies are about being empty-nesters; they are more about having grandchildren (or surrogates)—which I am pretty bad at. I think the seventies are about glorious freedom and the pleasure in little things and just gallivanting!

Until I was seventy and gained the 'aura', I never thought of myself as beautiful. The 'aura' means that everyone of every age is attracted—and I now stop to admire dogs and babies! I had never heard of the word 'granny arts' but I am just in admiration of friends who take up pottery or musical instruments. And my writing is better than ever. I was even asked out for dinner by a twenty-seven-year-old to talk about it.

I think the sixties are the years of 'zest' when people rush around doing things such as traveling, and the seventies are when you calm down and just do what you love doing."

Debbie Thawley, Canberra, Australia.

Chapter Three

Eunice Townsend

Memories of being twenty-one

Being active and looking fabulous are very important to Eunice, a self-described "seventy-nine year-old African-American woman." A former speech and language therapist, now retired for seventeen years, Eunice considers herself mature because she has finally admitted her age. Since retirement, Eunice has traveled extensively. She loves writing and is hoping to complete a book of poems and prose.

"Last night, I dreamt that I was twenty-one again, and life was just beginning to bloom. The skies of possibilities were forever blue, and the makings of love red hot. When I was young, I would see the applause in the eyes of passersby as I glided down the street dressed in confidence: youth has its own way of grabbing attention and admiration.

But I woke up and, with these memories lingering in my subconscious, actually sprang out of bed. When my feet landed on the floor, I was instantly reminded of the bilateral hip surgery I had undergone some years ago. Pain rose up, and my amnesiac body won the moment. *Okay, okay,* I thought, still holding on to a dream about to be shattered, *slow down—you're still in the game, not of youth, but of life.*

A shower seemed like a pleasant idea, but the water glazed over my somewhat bent body, and I noticed my breasts sleeping on my chest. 'Stand up,' I shouted, cupping both and pushing them upward. *Oh well, Victoria's Secret will have to assist me here,* I thought.

Putting on a dress that once showcased a svelte body and long legs, I was reminded of my age by a slight bulge around my once flat waist and legs that are marred with age spots. *I'll wear a belt to camouflage nights of ice cream and cake.*

Still holding on to the youthful image from my dream of last night, I went to the mirror to try to capture a reflection of a bygone face, now aged with lines and wrinkles. I felt sorrow rising when I realized that a neck that had never been noticed before, was now laden with pleated skin. *But I can don a scarf,* I think. *It's very fashionable now.*

At the mirror, I take out all my tools—moisturizer, foundation, concealer, blush for sunken cheeks, lipstick for disappearing lips, eyebrow pencil to liven up the appearance of my face, and last of all, mascara to open eyes that lie beneath hovering flesh.

My goodness, my hair has no body and it's so thin I can actually see my scalp. When did all these gray stands grow in my garden of hair? Oh my God, I look old, I don't want to look old. Looking old to some translates into lonely and forgotten. I am older, and sometimes I am lonely, but I am not forgotten.

Right then my granddaughter calls, 'Hey Granny, what we doing today?' And honey, I hurried up and put on my sunglasses and low heels and was out the door, happy to be feeling twenty-one once again."

Eunice Townsend, New Jersey, USA

Elena

"Ladies! Here is your last chance. Whatever was left unfinished from your sixties, now is the time to complete what you started. Before you know it, you will be eighty. So live your life in the best way possible, and do it now, one day at a time."

Cynthia

"I am a feral woman. I have become this way since my late sixties and see no reason to change in my early seventies. Whereas I used to cut and color my hair, wear makeup, and dress up, these days I see no reason to be anyone other than myself, unadorned—a version of myself in the 'wild'—and as a result, I have so much more time, time for myself!

With my husband, I moved several years ago from an urban center to a more remote although still civilized environment, and my response has been to change how I look and feel about myself. I like this new version of me. While I never imagined myself this way, I like who I am. My husband either hasn't noticed or doesn't mind—our priorities have changed. So I am who I am and that is how I plan to continue for the rest of my seventies and beyond."

Chapter Four

Zelda

When the parties stopped

A way of life that tied a marriage to a busy social life, with lots of hosting and entertaining, fades after a divorce. Perhaps there was just one more party to throw, one more reason to celebrate?

"My house was once the destination for many parties, fun events, and happy times. We would celebrate for almost any reason, for ourselves, and we were happy to share our home with others. 'We' was my husband and I.

My dining room—it's my dining room now, not 'our' dining room—is large, and lots of people can be seated at the expandable table I inherited from my grandmother. I own over thirty dining chairs of one sort or another; the spare chairs are stacked in the garage, but they haven't been used in over a year.

Daily, I walk past the extensive pantry and kitchen storage space that appealed to me when we purchased the house many years ago, but I seldom open the doors. I don't want to see those neatly organized dishes, dinner services (formal and casual), and endless glasses, glasses for all occasions: champagne flutes, red and white wine, port, and various sets of water glasses sitting in line like a regiment, called to order and now suspended before any deployment was initiated.

The parties stopped before my husband and I divorced; as our relationship slowly died, so did the desire for social events, all our friends gathered around the table as if nothing beneath the surface was happening, as if the discord and disconnect didn't exist. There are few table settings anymore—except for every other Thanksgiving, when my daughter and grandchildren visit and I ask old friends and neighbors to join us.

I've always liked parties because most people try to be someone else, at least for an hour or so—friendly and sociable, even if they do not feel that way—and part of me enjoys being part of this social game. Socializing on this scale also enabled me to get to know many people, but few people that I would come to know well, and that also suited me. But those large events, when friends brought dishes, there were place settings for everyone, and all had a good time—those times belong to a different era.

We were a classic gray divorce. We'd worn through each other, like favorite old clothes, thin in substance and not much use for anything but rags. Although it took time to admit it, we both wanted another shot at life in our late sixties—before it got to be too late. Too late for what, I can't say, but for whatever health issues the seventies and eighties would hold for us.

By divorcing, we decided not to be together for each other at that time, even after over forty years of marriage. We wanted to die apart, separate, potentially with other people, or alone. What does that say about our marriage?

He left, I stayed, unwilling to relinquish a house, a home, one that I was not ready to pack up. Selling up would feel like selling my identity, my past, and I was not prepared to let go of who I was, who I thought I was, as I am still trying to reconcile these different versions of myself.

Today, my ex-husband lives on the opposite coast in a new life. I don't know how it's going, and I am not about to ask, although I really would like to know, hoping for him that it's going well and at the same time not too well. I have not moved on in the way people recommend one should try. Going out, online dating, trying to meet new people hold no interest for me.

My daughter tells me that I am no different than a single woman in her twenties or thirties, staying home every night, making no effort to meet someone, yet hoping the perfect partner will magically show up at my door. 'It's a fantasy,' she chides me.

The thing is that in my early seventies, I have become someone else. Not the extraverted social person who would throw a party for any excuse. Your house isn't large enough—use mine. Do you have challenging family members visiting for the holidays? Add them to my party, and they will be diluted by the swell of people. Birthdays, anniversaries, and promotions, everyone is welcome. A cake, cake knives and plates, a couple of bottles of bubbly stuff—doesn't have to be the best; the bubbles are what count—and we have a party.

A quiet layer, like a thick heavily lined winter cloak, has descended on my house, and on my routines. The rhythms of the day are the distant sounds of traffic, a hum in the background, and my rituals of wake-up, caffeine, exercise, and then I check my to do list, varying the daily to-dos to extend the idea that I am busy.

I am, exactly, where I didn't want to be. If I could have pinpointed and described the place I wanted to be at seventy-two, this quiet life was the one thing I would have told you that I wanted to avoid.

I tell myself that I am thinking more, contemplating more, but the past is a version of events that we tell ourselves, often out of sequence, omitting many facts, reflecting varying perspectives, and distorting what we held to be true at the time.

I occupy a small corner of the house—living room, kitchen, bedroom—and the guest rooms are rarely used, while the dining room and pantry, scenes of great activity in the past, appear to be lost, forgotten, and forlorn.

It's clear that I should sell the house and find something smaller, possibly on one level, in anticipation of being less mobile in the future. But I am struggling with the prospect of sorting through all my dishes, glasses, formal and informal services, flatware, large serving pieces, and trays.

A friend suggested that I find an antique dealer to buy it all. Another suggested that I host a going-away party and invite friends, serve a meal, and then people can buy what they want, and I'll donate the proceeds to charity. If you like the decorative dinner plate you're eating on, you can buy it, buy the set, and the serving bowls to match!

But I don't want to part with all my things in that way, even though I'm willing to downsize. My daughter said she'd help me set up an online store, which my son-in-law, who is good at anything technical, will build, and then we'll sell all my things online.

I will become a woman with an identity, not just someone rattling around in a big house with too much stuff. I will be a woman who started a business in her seventies. My daughter tells me that there are plenty of people around the country who love vintage style who will happily buy my things, so I am going to learn to take photographs with my phone, improve my computer skills, and become a business woman.

Finally, I can see a purpose to having collected—and used—all my dishes, and perhaps what I needed was to find a purpose other than throwing parties; that is, helping other people to throw parties with my things.

Once everything is sold, I will downsize but I will be doing so on my own terms. Then, with an empty house, I'll turn up the music and invite everyone over—bring your own dishes—and we'll have one last party."

Gwen

"I feel almost giddy with excitement when I think about my seventies. I know that might sound strange as many women feel scared and disappointed when they reach their seventieth birthday. It's because I found my sixties to be puzzling. I didn't know who I was back then. But I'm an entirely new person in my seventies, and I'm loving it."

Chapter Five

Nancy Cahan

Life changes can open the heart

After a twenty-four-year marriage (twenty-nine years together), Nancy got divorced. With some trepidation, she started online dating, eventually met a match, and has been in a loving relationship for two and a half years. Nancy is seventy-three years old, still practicing psychology, and she is a ceramic artist.

"Our bodies change as we age, and it's quite an adjustment. I am active with yoga, bicycling, walking, and swimming, I feel fortunate to still be slender. However, gravity has its way as we age and embracing these changes can be challenging.

Even though I am active, I have scoliosis and stenosis of my spine that impact me at times, causing pain and discomfort. So, physical therapy here, maybe a cortisone shot there. It might have gotten worse over the years when I literally shrank three inches. I used to be tall. It feels like an ego blow, adjusting to letting go of the pride I felt being a tall woman. Not to psycho-ed too much, something I can't help given my profession, but we have to find ways to feel good about who we are, and not get hung up on the imperfect bodies and aching parts that we have.

Like many women, I had breast cancer (stage one), right before COVID-19 hit. I had a mastectomy of one breast. Fortunately, I did not have radiation or chemotherapy, but took anti-cancer meds for five years. I recently celebrated not having to take them anymore!

I am grateful that I am ok. I am also an artist, so the initial reconstruction of my breast (with an implant) was not just a bit disturbing but also fascinating. One breast was higher than the other, and the nipple peered out in a side position. I looked like one of Picasso's paintings. My breasts finally evened out, but after more years and the impact of gravity, which all aging women know, my natural breast is distinctly lower than the other breast. I feel fortunate that I never cared much about my breasts being perfect.

What I found through the surgery experience (first mastectomy, later reconstruction, then medication) was the importance of both feeling in control as much as possible in the face of something I didn't have much control over, and advocating for myself at every turn.

An example of this happened after being prepped for the reconstruction of my breast. As I was being wheeled into the operating room on a hospital bed, I chose to sit up, cross-legged, draped with that oh-so-nice heated blanket. Rather than feeling helpless, I felt a sense of calm and pride.

There have been many times in my life when I have not felt in control, which has made me anxious. Maybe it's because of being older and wiser that I permit myself to do what feels better in the moment, regardless of how I might appear to others.

At follow-up meetings over the next few years, I worked with my oncologist to change from one anti-cancer medication to another, and then to use half the dosage when the side effects interfered with my quality of life.

I realized that this is my life, and it's my choice how I want to live it. And how did I want to live it? No longer married to the man I was with for a large chunk of my life. Because I came from a childhood of emotional neglect and poor role-modeling, I was on my own from a young age—I became resourceful and independent, albeit with a tinge of underlying loneliness.

As I didn't really know what being in a loving partnership could be, what I deserved, or what was possible, I didn't expect much. We had children, I was busy being a mother, getting my doctorate, and over-functioning in the day-to-day. My ex-husband was not abusive; he had no addictions and did not cheat on me as far as I know, but I couldn't rely on him. In so many ways, he didn't show up for me, which made it hard for me to show up for him.

In retrospect, I realize that I never truly felt loved. Deeply tired of how I was over-functioning and not being emotionally met in our marriage, I asked my husband for change. He felt criticized, no matter how skillfully I tried to engage in a productive process.

We tried couples therapy to no avail. Parenthetically, as a couple's therapist, I have helped many couples establish a more loving connection. But I wasn't able to move the needle with us, so finally I asked for a divorce. It was agonizing to go through, but as soon as I had moved away, I felt an extraordinary sense of peace and gratitude. I had been grieving the relationship for many years and hadn't liked who I had become in it. I breathed free and felt relief.

At that point, I was ready for a relationship with a kind, considerate, emotionally intelligent man who shared my values, had a sense of humor, and someone I could enjoy good physical intimacy with. Someone I was attracted to, who cherished me, and whom I would love.

A lot to ask for, a 'needle in a haystack' I was told. Nonetheless, I started online dating. A fellow therapist quipped, 'You know it's a numbers game.' And it was.

I met fifty men over the course of a decade. I had five relationships, each lasting about three or four months, except for the first one, which lasted eighteen months. I was attracted to, smitten with, and felt in love with this man. I was hungry to love and be loved, to feel more alive with myself and someone else. There was so much that felt good at the beginning, but ultimately, I had to end the relationship as his narcissism and arrogance emerged more clearly. The signs were there at the beginning, but I ignored them.

Then there's the sex as we age. When menopause hits, many women struggle with not just vaginal atrophy (really, an awful term to be sure) but lower libido or total lack of sexual energy. I feel fortunate that I maintained my interest in physical intimacy. I found a product that my oncologist allowed, even with my estrogen-receptor-positive cancer.

Sex in later years is an adjustment for both men and women. It's an opportunity to open up to greater communication, acceptance, and focus on pleasure and creativity. Perhaps my active libido inspired me to stay with online dating, because that process is indeed an uncomfortable, sometimes weird experience to go through.

I became skilled at both letting a date know that I wasn't interested and managing my emotions if I was interested and they weren't. Even though I was happy enough with myself and didn't feel desperate, I didn't give up. At the age of seventy-one, I did find a man who met all the criteria. We are in a committed relationship that I trust. He shows up for me emotionally all the time. It is a delight to love and be loved, and sometimes it's a challenge for me to feel worthy of it, given my life experiences—but it's a wonderful challenge to have!

I feel that I have reached the best part of my life. In addition to my loving partner, I have deep friendships, ongoing creative work with ceramic sculpture, and a clinical practice that I enjoy, and I am in the process of whittling it down to allow for more travel with my partner and time for my studio artwork.

My body still allows me fluid movement and I am so appreciative. I recently became a member of the Human Rights Commission in my town, and it feels meaningful to be part of this group. I have adult children that I'm so proud of, and I am very happy that they are doing well in life. I live in a beautiful town near the ocean, and I'm open to making new friends and having experiences that awaken my heart and spirit.

In my yoga classes, the poet Mary Oliver is read, particularly the poem that ends with the line, 'Tell me, what is it you plan to do with your one wild and precious life?'

The truth is that I, we, are closer to death. Mortality cannot be denied. No one is immune. My own brush with cancer was a wake-up call for me, and I know many people who struggle with illnesses and losses. I have learned that age has nothing to do with the capacity to love, and being open to vulnerability is an important ingredient."

Nancy Cahan, Psy,D., Massachusetts, USA.

Chapter Six

Anne

Unfinished business

A sense of something being incomplete had occupied Anne throughout her life. In her seventies, she finally understood and resolved the feeling in an unexpected way.

"Something has nagged at me for most of my life, tugged at my thoughts in the background of daily life. For years, it was difficult to describe the feeling, to identify it, but it was as if there was, at my core, a sense of unease, of unfulfillment, or restlessness even, as if I had left something undone.

I pushed it aside. Life was busy with activities, limiting time for self-reflection. I was married, had a son, and had a busy working life.

The feeling didn't bother me in everyday life back then, but after I was divorced from my husband, retired, and spent a lot of time alone, I had to acknowledge that a sense of something in my life was unfinished, or perhaps not yet started. If I am honest, I found it hard to know the difference.

I've just turned seventy-one. I've been single for over a decade. Our only son recently moved to Canada from the USA to join his Canadian-born wife. They are expecting their first child. I feel more alone now than ever before, not least because my daughter-in-law has a large and involved family in Canada. I feel excluded by more than just distance, which always involves a change of planes as there are no direct flights, and it takes a long time to reach the destination where I always feel, at best, an outsider. Although I am happy for my son, I would have liked him to be closer to me.

I still have good friends in the town where I live now, but there are upcoming changes, with friends talking of moving away, of finding their 'forever home,' which I think of as their last home. I thought they were living in their 'forever home,' but it turns out the yard is too much to manage, and no one wants to go up and down stairs anymore.

Friends have died, sadly, those we thought most likely to survive all of us, but their premature deaths act as puncture wounds—often unexpected—in our reality, reminders that life strikes at us whether we are ready or not. We don't get to choose.

Sometimes, I think social media reads my mind. One night, sitting on the sofa with a program on the TV that didn't really interest me, I began surfing on my phone. There isn't any advice anywhere in the world suggesting that phone surfing is a good thing to do, yet many of us do it, whether we like to admit it or not.

I feel really conflicted about this. Part of me enjoys the things the algorithms serve up to me, and at other times, I am shocked that the algorithms think I might be interested in specific topics. It feels like a playground of text and images, flung against the screen's wall, in hopes of catching my attention.

At other times, it just seems as if everything we've even glimpsed or spent a few seconds watching is served back up at us ten fold in various formats. Like everyone else, I've clicked on new kitchen pans, gardening equipment, and a skin care product. And for the next five or six days—is there a timeline, I wonder?—every time I am online, I am shown multiple things to buy based on my brief interest.

Suddenly, for a reason I have yet to understand—what was the prompt?—the screen started filling up with images of Tuscan villas and French country houses: not mansions and chateaux, but small houses, many of them in need of renovation, in remote hilltop or countryside villages.

How could the internet know, and be able to interpret, my deepest thoughts, even thoughts I had yet to identify? Something tugged at me when looking at those images, triggering that sense of something missing, and in no time at all, my mind started fantasizing about moving.

I couldn't pinpoint the moment, but it happened suddenly. I had a mission. The TV program entirely forgotten, I moved from my phone to my laptop and started to look for blogs and articles about moving to Europe.

My interest in changing my life—in a drastic way—turned into an obsession. I read for hours on end, hunting down information about the pros and cons of an American moving to Europe, buying a home, and retiring there.

For months, I kept everything to myself. I held my dreams in my arms—the combination of excitement and potential—feeling that it was too much, overwhelming, to share with anyone else. I didn't say a word to my son or to my friends. Not until I had a plan. I didn't want anyone to burst the bubble I had created for myself.

I loved hugging this secret, wrapping it around me like a embrace, a warm embrace, and it felt good. An energy that I didn't know I was lacking returned to me, and I found enthusiasm in the most mundane of things.

My son, on a phone call, asked me if I'd met someone because I sounded so 'bubbly.' Part of me was shocked that he would ask me such a question, and the other part was affronted that it would take 'meeting someone' to change my attitude.

After six months, I started talking about my plans to my friends, and, predictably, my ideas were met disbelief and shock. One friend was supportive, but most others got caught up in the logistics of how I was going to accomplish this feat, as one friend described it, and the legal and financial aspects.

Several friends mentioned that small homes in Europe are often built over several stories. What would I do with stairs, possibly slippery stone steps? Feeling alone in this venture didn't dampen my excitement—quite the opposite, it fueled my decision.

A year after this all started, I called my son in Canada and told him of my plans. Although I had yet to settle on the country, let alone on a house, I wanted him to know what I was thinking. He had many questions, but fortunately, I had many answers.

We discussed what I would do with my property in the USA, and he asked me if I would first consider renting out my house and renting a home in Italy or Portugal—I still hadn't entirely decided—for six months or a year to see if it would suit me.

I am in the process of picking a country. My goal is to take a crash course in Italian or Portuguese, pick a town, then a house, and move, renting out my home in Ohio in the process. If it sounds reckless, it isn't; it's all well-planned.

But I can't see into the future. I don't know what is going to happen, but the sense of unease I've always felt is starting to fade. What I need now, what I've needed all along, I've realized, is an adventure in my life, one big adventure, a significant risk in a life where they have been so few risks.

Although it's taken me all this time—these years—to realize it, I've finally gotten to this point. I'm moving to another country for a year—or maybe for a lifetime—but however long it is, I am determined to have the adventure of my life. Wish me luck."

Margot

"While my friends complained about turning seventy, I felt some relief at my seventieth birthday. The second-to-last decade had arrived, and I was ready for it. I closed out my sixties with big plans for my seventies. With time pressing on me, the sense of urgency I felt was neither unpleasant nor discomforting. I felt I'd come to terms with just about everything, and I was ready to move forward with all my plans for the decade."

"During my sixties, I had several health issues, but I am happy to say that I am currently healthy and plan to stay that way. I have always been a happy person, one who believes we are responsible for our own happiness, and I've maintained a positive attitude throughout my life.

What I learned from my sixties, and what I will carry into these next years, is that contentment is my only remaining goal. I want peace and contentment more than anything. I want to be able to sit on my porch and listen to birds chirp while feeding off the birdfeeders, to water my plants and flowers and then just sit and absorb their beauty. I want to have my grandchildren come and visit and for us all to go swimming together, to have dinner with friends, to go to the movies, and to read every book the library will lend to me. I want to live and enjoy life, and I am the only one who can make that happen; that's what being in my seventies means for me."

Amanda Stanton, Texas, USA.

Eleanor

"Growing up I was trained to please people, and never to disappoint. I've spent most of my life trying to accommodate others, my parents, my husband, my children, and my friends. In my sixties, free from responsibilities, I struggled with identity, unwilling to fully accept my life, living in an world without constraints. But in my seventies I'm finding the person I once glimpsed in my twenties. She's there, still inside me, ready to be formed and shaped into the person I want to be now. My last chance! It's not too late."

Chapter Seven

Kathleen Chamberlin

Stepping out from behind self-judgment

Being risk-averse and fearing rejection are powerful forces in preventing someone from achieving their goals. In Kathleen's case, she saw herself in life only as a "'would-be" writer, lacking the courage to seek publication of her work. But life—and the encouragement of two friends—changed all that.

"Walt Disney once said, 'All our dreams can come true if we have the courage to pursue them.' Sadly, I did not have the courage, and if you're like me, you stood on the sidelines and marveled at the achievers, the people who put in the hours, wrote novels, and who took risks.

Those people seemed to dwell on a mountaintop, out of reach, while I, an introverted 'would-be' writer, remained below, at the foot of the mountain, yearning to have their kind of courage. And I'm sure I'm not the only woman whose insecurities prevented her from trying, convinced that her writing was merely mediocre.

It didn't make any difference to me that my English teachers had praised my writing. That was a private matter: I made a humble offering before the shrine of academia and was rewarded. But I never thought of those grades as earned, just bestowed by benevolent judges—so I kept my writing to myself. I was a closet poet, a writer of short stories and philosophical musings that almost no one else knew about.

And so it went, from year to year. After college, I became an educator, entering each classroom, every semester, armed with Shakespeare, Hawthorne, Emerson, and Poe, and I taught my heart out, always hearing the mantra: 'Those who can, do. Those who can't, teach.'

After I retired, I wrote vignettes about people I knew. I wrote poems to lost loves, or poems to harness anger or hurt. I wrote plot ideas in a notebook, like Hawthorne did, and I wrote a series of first lines that I thought were solid invitations to the world I wanted to create. I kept them all in a folder, in my desk drawer, nestled against my old tax returns.

They might have remained there, but then the world changed. COVID-19 rampaged across America, and mortality loomed large in my consciousness. Had I fulfilled my life's purpose? Did I have unfinished business? Would I leave the planet with regrets?

My best friend and I had been challenging each other with life questions since seventh grade. As we both turned seventy-two, the questions took on a deeper significance. I had only shared my writing with her, until, by chance, I reconnected with someone whom I hadn't heard from in fifty years. While catching up, I mentioned my passion for writing but said I had never tried to get my work published. The response was: 'Why not?'

Why not, indeed. It was now or never. I pulled out my folder, gathered some stories and poems, and sent them off to find homes in publications. I want to say that my work met with instant success, but that wasn't the case. Six rejections followed in rapid succession.

Then, an email arrived. I read it four times: my poem had been accepted for publication. As excited as I was, the demons of doubt whispered to me that the only reason the poem had been accepted was that it was short and would fill the space at the bottom of the magazine's page.

Nevertheless, I shared the news with the two people who had urged me to submit my work and basked in their approval and encouragement. 'Congratulations; keep trying,' they said. 'You're on your way.'

I felt alive! I went back to the drawing board, edited old poems, and wrote new ones. Although the rejections kept coming, an email finally arrived addressed to 'Dear Poet.' A second poem accepted! Two short story acceptances followed. Feeling elated, I acknowledged a change in myself:

I was no longer stymied by my own fears. Each triumph was shared with my two cheerleaders. More acceptances arrived, and I'm proud to say they now number one hundred and twenty-six.

I know I owe my modest success to the two people who encouraged me—make no mistake, the word encouragement has 'courage' embedded within it. By taking risks, I exposed myself to rejection, but as a result, in my seventies, I have the enormous satisfaction of sharing my words with many people.

Today, I am no longer a 'would-be' writer but happily think of myself as a fledgling writer with more to share with the world, proving that age should never be viewed as an impediment or a stop sign. As long as we draw breath, we can turn our dreams into reality."

Kathleen Chamberlin, New York State, USA.

Chapter Eight

Margaret Johnson

A renewed sense of community after profound loss

From meeting a new community in her sixties when learning to dance (inspired by Isadora Duncan), to experiencing the profound loss of a beloved sister in her seventies, Margaret's life continues to expand with people and creativity. Honoring her sister with a book has become her latest project, putting Margaret in touch with a new group of people, something she never imagined at a stage in life when many people's worlds are shrinking.

"I have never been goal-oriented. I have backed into all my careers and life events, and it has worked well for me. I am still working (independent picture researcher) and pursuing my own creative projects. That said, I have noticed a slowing down, and I am cautious about going downstairs. But what has slowed me down—age, or circumstance?

When I turned seventy-one, it was the beginning of the COVID-19 shutdown; literally, life as we knew it changed. Activities and tempo ground to a halt.

And when I was seventy-two, my sister—my North Star—died. Her illness had spanned seven years. She had some good, strong years during that time, but when she had surgery and treatments, I was there.

Neither COVID-19 nor grief is age-related. COVID-19 may have been a gift for me. It made life simpler as I grieved the loss of my sister.

Many people in their seventies experience a shrinking social circle and loneliness. That isn't my experience. Of course, I was isolated and disengaged during COVID-19 and the rawness of early grief after my sister died, but once those ebbed, my life returned to something I recognized as normal.

My work is solitary because I am a freelancer, which I like. But I seek community elsewhere. At sixty, I started studying Isadora Duncan's technique and discovered a vibrant, local, national, and international dance community. Movement, laughter, and challenges are always good.

And now, I am working on a book about my sister, another project I backed into. I needed to sort through her closets, deciding what to keep, toss, or donate. She had some wonderful things that she hoped could be studied for their cut, texture, and design. And then her friends showed up—people I didn't know. What started as a tedious and sad task turned into many creative sessions with her friends, who are now my friends. Fast forward: her clothes are in a fashion archive, and the book is being printed.

Community is good."

Margaret Johnson, Washington DC, USA.

Mary

"There's one elemental truth about the seventies that most people forget every minute, hour, and day that they are walking on the planet. Time is a luxury. We all take it for granted. And we never think about it until someone we love is gone, or a health issue threatens our own viability. Time should never be taken for granted."

"I think regrets come with just being human. It is often not until we look back in our rearview mirror of time passing that we decide whether an experience has left us so unfulfilled that we put it into the category of 'regret.'

I try not to hold regretful things as much as I try to understand the process, the teachings, and whether forgiveness is needed. Forgiveness is a complex topic, and I am unable to answer the question of forgiveness easily.

Sometimes, things happen beyond our control. Forgiveness isn't always immediate or possible. Through one experience, I learned that giving myself permission to walk forward was the best that I could do—allowing the past hurt to soften with time and leaving space for forgiveness to emerge. I am accountable only to myself and the peace in my heart. An examined life comes with deep introspection, which is never-ending."

Constance Soutullo, Florida, USA.

Chapter Nine

Lucia Cavalcanti de Albuquerque

We get to decide when we feel old

After losing two sisters who were in their early thirties, Lucia believes that it is a privilege to grow old. She is aging with a healthy body, an active brain, and sufficient energy. She continues to be curious about the world, learning something new each day, finding awe in nature, art, and humanity. She is seventy-five, and she doesn't feel old.

"Recently, one of my grandchildren asked his parents if they had felt old when they turned forty. How relative time is; my memory quickly jumped back to the early nineties, when I certainly did not feel old on my fortieth birthday. Instead, I remember feeling a special kind of maturity—I had achieved a distinctive landmark of adulthood.

At the time, I was trying to become a registered psychologist in my adopted country of Canada. As a single mother of three young children, I hated the English expression, much in use at the time, of a 'broken home.' My family was certainly not broken!

I was lucky enough to live at a time when women could choose divorce rather than living unhappily for the rest of their lives. Besides, I had joint custody. My ex-husband, a former colleague and the children's father, lived a few blocks away on the same Toronto street. The children resided with me but saw their father regularly. There were challenges, of course, but separating was an initiative that I never regretted.

When I turned fifty, I was back in my birth country of Brazil. My ex-husband had accepted a position at an American university, and the joint custody arrangement had become unfeasible.

Thus, I decided to return to Brazil with my children to be near my parents, who were still healthy in their early seventies. It was the least I could do for my parents, who had given my sisters and me a blissful childhood.

I then resumed a university career, working in the same department where my Canadian husband and I had taught before moving to Toronto.

At the time of my fiftieth birthday, I did not feel old, a sentiment that was reinforced by a lovely card I received from my eldest son, who wrote something like, 'When I look at you now at fifty, I sometimes see the same girl as in your childhood pictures.'

And I definitely did not feel old when I turned sixty, although by then I had legally become a senior in Brazil. I celebrated this milestone of a birthday at a patio restaurant on a Honolulu beach. By then, I had become a successful researcher in family violence prevention, which allowed me to interact with interesting colleagues and to fly to conferences around the world.

How can you feel old on a Hawaiian beach? I was collaborating on a project with an Australian colleague who was attending the same conference, and she had arranged for a restaurant dinner to celebrate my birthday with some of her Aussie colleagues and her husband.

My daughter, who was pursuing her master's degree in England, sent me a gift that included a special tour and shopping, which I took at the end of the conference. As a result of that trip, I still possess a beautiful seashell choker and a Hawaiian cushion.

By the time I turned seventy, I had moved again, after retirement, to Canada's capital city, Ottawa. By then, all three of my children were working in Canada, my sons in Toronto and my daughter in Ottawa. My youngest son asked me how I wished to celebrate my birthday, and I replied that I wanted to go to Paris with the entire family.

It was wishful thinking, of course. My Brazilian pension could not stretch to afford the extravagance, and, even if it could, the world had just come to a halt due to the COVID-19 pandemic. But we were allowed to meet in our own bubbles, particularly if we had a small party in an open space.

My family organized an unforgettable luncheon at the gazebo in the gardens of my condo. Around noon, I heard a feeble knock at my door: my grandkids, dressed as miniature airplane pilots, aviator hats included, had arrived to escort me to Paris!

The gazebo was decorated with French flags and a poster of the Eiffel Tower. French music provided a fitting backdrop as we enjoyed the treats lovingly found by my daughter at a local patisserie: croissants, brioche, madeleines, macarons, eclairs, and a variety of cheeses and French wine, of course.

I don't remember feeling old then, despite knowing that this next decade would bring new challenges to my health when my body would begin to show a new vulnerability to pain, sometimes in the knees, the back, even in the fingers or the wrists.

When I say that I didn't feel old, that doesn't mean that I was in denial, then or now, when I looked at myself in the mirror. I certainly knew that as the decades passed, my face and body continued to age. But despite looking like a mature woman with gray hair, I don't feel old in the sense that I am extremely joyful to be alive.

However, I have experienced how seniors become invisible to youth. For example, I was once sitting in an airplane aisle seat next to a young couple. When it was time for the young male flight attendant to serve lunch, he first chatted a bit with the couple. He then gave each of my neighbors a tray and departed, leaving me empty-handed. To obtain my lunch, I had to stand up and say, with a dry smile, 'Hey, I also exist.'

But these small frustrations have more to do with others than with my own aging process. My grandparents died in their sixties and seventies, and my parents in their eighties. So it is probable that I will outlive them, particularly because scientific knowledge continually improves our quality of life and our chances of survival. My parents did not know, for example, that seniors cannot thrive living a sedentary life. And the cycle will continue: my children and grandchildren will experience many of the benefits of the science of gerontology that I will not.

To keep fit, my exercise routine involves YouTube yoga first thing in the morning—a must because it keeps me calm, and my body begs for all those stretches. As a result, I see positive transformation in an aging body, such as my feet becoming more rooted and my posture improving.

I use the stairs rather than the elevator to reach my fifth-floor condo, a suggestion I read decades earlier in the book *French Women Don't Get Fat,* and I take daily walks around my neighborhood.

Medical evidence proves that this routine is working. A year ago, I had a bad case of fasciitis. As I was not recovering, my physician referred me to a specialist to conduct a muscle exam to detect any other possible problems. I then went to a university medical clinic where a technician connected electrodes to my leg.

Afterward, a physician came to examine me and present the results. He was a friendly man in his early fifties who smiled and said, 'The technician told me that you had the best muscle results of the day,' adding, 'When I grow up, I want to be like you.'

I thanked him. 'So, there is nothing wrong with my feet?'

He asked me if I walked barefoot at home and recommended that I always wear shoes inside the house. He said, 'Your fasciitis will be gone soon. Keep up the good work.'

Exercising is, of course, just one strong component of a to-do list that goes on and on. For example, eating a healthy diet, not smoking, not drinking, sleeping well, forming positive social interactions, and, of course, enjoying projects. I can't simply retire, sit, and look at a screen.

I loved my academic life, but retired not only because I moved countries but also because it was an opportunity to embrace a new career as a writer.

I completed a book recounting how my Brazilian family faced the tragic deaths of two of my sisters, (one by femicide and another while waiting for a heart and lung transplant) by joining forces and raising four children with much love and affection.

Presently, I am writing a second book, a biography of an artist who was my grandmother's cousin. She sculpted the hands of Christ the Redeemer, a statue that is considered to be one of the wonders of the modern world, in Rio de Janeiro. But nobody knows about this incredible feat, as women are generally not recognized for their accomplishments. I inherited four large boxes of her photographs and scrapbooks, and the research has been fascinating. My research has also led me to meet a distant cousin living in the USA, with whom I've shared wonderful memories.

After I finish book two, I plan to write two additional books, but then I think I will retire for good. Most certainly, I will no longer be climbing stairs. Perhaps, by then, I will feel old. We will see."

Lucia Cavalcanti de Albuquerque, Ottawa, Canada.

Claire

"I'm not seventy years old, I'm seventy years young. That's how I look at it. I struggle to understand why people think seventy is old. So many people I know—particularly women—are thriving in this decade. We may be a little less mobile and may need a little more sleep, but we have thrown off the expectations of this decade and we're ready to embrace our next decade."

Laura

"Treasure your vanity. It might be the thing that keeps you going through the seventies when we struggle to live up to our own expectations. Hang on to your pride and self-admiration, because over the next two decades, as your body and your mind deteriorate, you will need them."

Chapter Ten

Angela

Dressing up and dressing down

A closet full of clothes that no longer seem to fit a lifestyle—and her changing body shape— was the reality of Angela's life. She believes that she is not the only woman in her seventies with wardrobe dilemmas, or the only one with clothes for a life she no longer leads.

"It's taken decades for me to come to terms with my clothes: what I buy, what suits me, and what I wear out in public rather than the clothes I lounge around in at home, although, if I'm honest, those demarcation lines have blurred.

It started in my fifties when I gained weight that I found difficult to lose, and my shape has continued to change, and not in a good way.

It doesn't help that I don't feel alone with this problem. While I can find lots of information online to help 'women like me,' the truth is that I don't care about the weight problems of other women. For me, it is genetic, at this stage in life I look like my mother and grandmother, and while I wear different clothes, my shape resembles theirs at the same age.

In my sixties, it became clear to me that I had a wardrobe full of clothes I'd never had the opportunity to wear, because every day I lived in one form or another of Lycra and a cotton T-shirt in summer, and swapped the T-shirt for a sweatshirt in winter. It wasn't as if I was going to the gym or working out—just walking as exercise—but I wanted to look the part and, possibly, like everyone else, it was just easy to reach for these clothes every day. I didn't have to think about it.

Sadly though, it doesn't matter how many athletic-style clothes I buy and wear; I still do not look as fit as I would like people to see me.

COVID-19 really did change everything in the world when it came to dressing. If you had no where to go except a room with a computer screen to attend a meeting or a Zoom call with family and friends or work, did it matter what you wore?

In my view, we lost something—a sense of style, perhaps to the point at which women today who dress as they once did pre-pandemic now look oddly out of place, as if they reverted to pre-2020 dress. They haven't adapted their style to a less structured, less proscribed look that has been widely influential. I don't want to be frozen in time in terms of style.

I know I am not the only woman who has bought clothes for occasions that I have yet to be invited to. For example, the long black tailored wool coat, designer label, purchased on sale, that I could wear to a funeral, except that the only funerals and memorial services I attended took place in spring, summer, and fall, so the coat has never been worn.

A dress, red—what was I thinking; red isn't even good for my skin tone—that I could wear to a gala event. The last gala event I attended was over twenty years ago. I wore something covered in sequins that I couldn't get past my shoulders today.

A conservative blue dress; this was when I was interviewing for jobs, except that all the interviews took place over a computer screen. I am not a conservative person, so why would I think I would fit in anyway? It's probably a good thing I didn't get the job.

Then there was my hippie phase. In my late sixties, I downsized and I tried to sell or donate my more structured clothes—some, admittedly, I'd had for years, including custom-made cocktail dresses—but no one was buying that look.

At the consignment store, the young clerk was nice. She politely implied that my clothes were from a 'different' era and were unlikely to sell to her customer base, as she indicated all the young women shopping in the store, none of whom looked as if they would ever wear my clothes. Many were pushing infants in strollers.

The clerk asked whether any of the clothes were from the eighties or nineties, and if so, I might consider the vintage store.

Sadly, without the prerequisite designer labels, the vintage store wasn't interested either, so I remember angrily shoving them back in my closet, trying hard not to think of all the money I'd spent. My daughter suggested we cut them down, and her daughters—my granddaughters—might use them for dress up; in other words, my clothes would become costumes.

It's accurate to say I lost my style in the decade of my sixties, and it's still missing. I am not sure why I cared so much because I felt invisible for most of this decade, something that has not changed now in my seventies. Did it matter then, what I wore? It mattered to me.

I've tried. I have spent hours online looking at blogs and images of 'styles for older women.' Much of the information made me uncomfortable because, if I am honest with myself—and this is difficult to admit—I've made many errors in dress style over the decades, not just recently.

For my birthday, my daughter gifted me with a 'color' consultant, with whom I discovered that I am a Bright Winter, which confirmed that most of the clothes in my wardrobe will not, have not, and will never suit me. I've been buying clothes for a Spring or Summer woman.

With my color palette tucked into my purse, I am starting over, shopping thrift stores, vintage stores, and sales (online and instore) as I am rebuilding my wardrobe.

I've encouraged several friends to get their 'colors done,' and as a result, we are now swapping clothes—over wine—and laughing about the mistakes we've made in the past and happily gifting each other clothes that no longer suit us.

Two questions linger. One, why did I wait until my seventies to do this, and two, why do this in my seventies when I spend more time at home than ever before? It's not as if I suddenly have places to go in my new clothes.

Here are my answers. I've made a pledge to myself. I don't want to be remembered as 'granny' who wore large, baggy, shapeless clothes in weird colors with odd bits of jewelry that I thought defined me (and it turns out everyone else thought looked bizarre).

I've also visited a hair color consultant, and I have been persuaded to part with my blonde curls. I can see now that the color was all wrong for me—too blonde, too brassy, and unsuitable for my complexion—and that I was chasing a vision of myself that really didn't impress anyone but me. Was I still trying to turn heads with this look? And what would someone see? An aging woman with a head full of blonde curls. Maybe some women can pull this look off—but not me.

That was a hard reconciliation. When you have attended multiple events thinking you looked great, when most people were thinking, *Why does she color her hair that way?*, and when friends said, 'Oh, you've had your hair done,' but not 'Your hair looks great,' I realized that I was simply drawing attention to myself, but that no one appreciated what they were seeing. It was all in my mind.

For anyone reading this who might be inclined to say, 'You should just be yourself,' or thinking or saying the 'You do you' statement, I would say this. I am 'doing me.' Asking for, paying for, and receiving help about skin tone and clothing colors, albeit later in life, has been one of the best things I've done.

Being honest with yourself hurts. Not everyone is willing to put themselves under a microscope for dissection that may reveal hard truths, but with this comes freedom and, with the opportunity presented by a new decade, to start anew.

I may not have that many more years on this planet, but I want to live those years as well-dressed (for me) as possible. And armed with a newly found confidence, and some compliments, I don't care what anyone else thinks."

Sarah

"Growing up, every year, my parents purchased a new coat for me to wear in winter which, in the UK, can last from October through April. There was always excitement about this coat, the style, buttons, pockets and collar, as well as much discussion about what color was 'in' and what color was considered 'out.' The new coat was considered to be my 'good' coat, to be used for 'best' occasions.

My other coat was relegated to secondary status, to be worn on a daily basis. Today, my closet is full of coats of all kinds, for all seasons and reasons. But a 'good' coat, for 'best'? Any coat that works for the occasion is the 'best' coat. I have too many coats. I got rid of some of my coats, for no other reason than I go out less. I don't need a 'best' coat. A coat is something you take off when you arrive and put on when you leave."

Sue

"The other day, I caught sight of myself in a full-length mirror. While I have a full-length mirror at home, I never look at myself from the side. I was shocked at how my posture had changed. Not only did I look older, but I was hunched over; I looked like an older version of myself, but not the version I had expected. I looked more like my grandmother in build and in height than I did like my mother. This, too, was unexpected.

Silly, isn't it, to think I would have a vision of myself in mind as to how I would age. If I weren't so disappointed by my appearance, I would have laughed at myself. But I see this as an opportunity. I can work on my posture so that next time I see myself—sideways—I will be proud of the woman I have become."

Chapter Eleven

Ermelinda Mancini

Overcoming childhood trauma

A self-described immigrant child, and the eldest of six, from a young age, Ermelinda was relied upon to act as a parent, caretaker, bill-payer, and interpreter. In her view, she had a classic case of Eldest Daughter Syndrome, with responsibilities that stunted her emotional growth. Hampered by her strict upbringing, naivete, and isolation, she didn't realize when someone tried to take advantage of her.

"It's uncanny how the numbers seventy-one and seventeen both have the same digits in them, only in reverse. 'Seven' is supposed to be a lucky number, and 'one' is the loneliest number. When I was seventeen, I suffered a traumatic experience.

At that age, I was desperately lonely and alone, all the while surrounded by family, friends, and neighbors. I could not have known that what I understood as kind deeds and gestures from one of my supervisors were actually ways to take advantage of an innocent, unsuspecting teen. A predator was grooming me. All these years, I have kept quiet about it, and now, at seventy-one, I am only just getting to grips with what transpired and finally talking about it.

Today, the burden I have shouldered all these years is lighter to bear, but before now, I had buried the incident in the far reaches of my mind, hoping it would disappear.

While therapy has helped, it has not erased the memory, and I will never be able to relieve myself of the load I carry. But I feel liberated because I no longer blame myself for what happened.

Why am I only realizing this in my seventies? Why do I now feel empowered and invincible? I can only assume that, at my age, criticism doesn't matter any more and I am not concerned about what others think.

Loved ones whom I sheltered from the truth to save myself are no longer on this earth, and those who are have dementia. It was my cross to bear, and I bore it alone, never once realizing that help was available. Initially silenced by fear and shame, I am now determined to ensure my voice is heard.

The word 'grooming' was not in our lexicon back in the 1970s, unless you were referring to making oneself neat and tidy. Sexual grooming, as we know now, is the action or behavior used to establish an emotional connection with a vulnerable person—generally a minor under the age of consent. The 'Me Too' social movement and awareness campaign against sexual abuse, sexual harassment, and rape culture, changed all that.

But for me, it came too little, too late. The movement allowed women to emerge from behind a curtain of shame, realizing that they were pawns in a vicious game and were not to blame for what happened. The voices of these women are now being heard.

How did this happen? As an immigrant child and the eldest of six, I was expected to help around the home.

Beginning at age nine, when twins joined the family, my parents entrusted me with huge responsibilities. Eldest Daughter Syndrome, as it has come to be known, is a pattern of behavior and expectations placed on the eldest daughter in a family, leading to increased duties that also create an emotional toll.

Household chores, childcare, emotional support for siblings, and setting good examples are just a few of the syndrome's characteristics.

The eldest daughter in an immigrant family also assumes the responsibilities of interpreter for medical appointments and parent/teacher interviews, as well as writing checks to pay bills. Oftentimes, the roles assigned to eldest daughters are overwhelming, and they disrupt healthy development, leading to long-term psychological effects. The childhood of these eldest daughters is lost.

As such, I felt compelled to lead, to be the role model, to excel at what I did, and to pave the path for my siblings moving forward. What kind of an example would I have set if I had revealed my horrific experience? It was easier to bottle everything up.

Obedience was another controlling factor, and for me, that meant that my parents chose my husband for me. In this arranged marriage—I was only nineteen—we were allowed one year of courtship before marrying. And in another numerical coincidence, my first marriage lasted for seventeen years, and it was mostly fraught with tears.

Now, I have been blessed with a kind, caring, and loving partner, who sings my praises even when none are due. My two daughters live in the same city as I do, and, while they are busy with their own lives, we can easily get together when time allows. Four grandchildren bring me enormous joy, and I pamper and spoil them in ways that I never did for my own children at that age.

In my early seventies, I came to realize that the number 'seven' has been a good number for me, and that the number 'one' is no longer a lonely number.

I am *numero uno,* and I am living life to the fullest, without having to answer to anyone, without hiding, without worrying, without shame, and without remorse. There are no limitations on my life, no time constraints. I do what I want, when I want, if I want, and with whom I wish to. I am free to spread my wings and soar.

Sadly, the wings have osteoporosis, and the knee joints are arthritic. My libido is non-existent; I'm fatigued or not in the mood, or both.

I still turn heads, which surprises me with my Arctic blonde hair, as one kind hairdresser referred to it when he was styling my snow-white, yellow-streaked mane. He was quick to point out that if I used the proper shampoo, the yellow would disappear. But I am convinced that heads turn because I am a blonde, so the yellow stays.

I will no longer follow hairdressers' recommendations or spend hundreds of dollars on products that sit dormant under my bathroom sink.

Recently, a kind woman who is no doubt waiting for cataract surgery told me I looked the youngest of my six siblings.

And on a standing-room-only bus recently, a young lady occupying the priority seating reserved for the elderly or disabled offered me the seat. I declined her kind offer, but she insisted. I presumed she took me for a senior until she asked me when I was due.

I have the worst posture imaginable, especially when I am exhausted, as was the case on the bus. My bloated upper belly is more pronounced when I slouch and makes me look like I am in my last trimester of pregnancy. My clothes seem to emphasize rather than camouflage my round belly. Although I should have been upset that the young lady assumed I was pregnant, in retrospect, I am beaming that she thought I was young enough to conceive still. At the time, I accepted the seat she vacated.

I try to stay active with pickleball and a weekly golf game, but the thrill of both activities diminishes when women our age form little cliques and you find yourself either in their circle or outside of it, in which case you are only called upon when a spare person is needed. I prefer to leave them high and dry and with their threesomes. I guess you could say I cut off my nose to spite my face, as the saying goes, but so be it.

This is a new me at seventy-one, and I'm loving it! It's so much better than being seventeen."

Ermelinda Mancini, Ontario, Canada.

Moira

"If I had to find one word to describe how I am living my seventies, I would say it is with 'grace.' My sixties were a confusing time, and I was uncertain of myself and life in general, but by the time I reached seventy, I'd discovered an inner confidence and resilience."

Chapter Twelve

Chyrell Botts

Retreading ground to move forward

Entering her seventies, Chyrell felt as if she was emerging from hibernation to encounter familiar things and places, only now she was looking at everything through a different lens—one framed in positivity and appreciation. She has rediscovered her creativity and her love of travel, and she has sought out new ways to enrich her life.

"My seventies began with a burst of energy and an immense longing to travel again.

My entire young adult life was spent in Europe, where I studied, worked, traveled extensively, and pursued art.

The middle years of my life, back in the United States, were spent educating young college students from vulnerable socioeconomic backgrounds who were struggling to get an education. Although I kept my hand in both art and travel, there was really little time or opportunity to pursue them as I had before.

With complete retirement, I found myself eager to learn new things, to get back into art, hone my skills, and let art encompass me as I could now give it my full attention. Diving back into traveling was also a priority, but this time with a different set of eyes and a new inner life.

One of the most interesting aspects of the early seventies has been realizing how much you have grown and learned over the years, so that your trips are now experienced with greater depth and insight. The fun and excitement are still there, but the experiences have changed.

I went to India for the first time in 1981, and except for the first few months, I traveled basically alone throughout that vast country for around five months. It was a life-changing experience.

I returned to India in 2019, thirty-eight years later, at the age of seventy-two. I cannot say that it was a life-changing experience at that point, but I can say that it was profoundly interesting, with many changes, while at the same time remaining essentially the same as before. Recognizing what has remained gives one a deeper understanding of, and insight into, a people—these things I find interesting.

My creative life took on a new energy in my early seventies. It was as if I had awakened from a long hibernation. I wanted to work with a new medium and take a break from painting for a while. I took some courses in ceramic sculpture and loved the tactile experience.

At the same time, I took a college-level geography course. Having never studied geography in college, I was eager to learn about the Earth and its formations while working with clay. I found myself taking information and concepts I was learning about and translating them into clay sculptures. Different crystals, formed by the slow cooling of molten rock inside the Earth or through the evaporation of water in mineral-rich solutions, were expressed in a set of semi-abstract sculptures. This was really good fun.

The missing pieces of this endeavor were revealed to me when I saw an exhibition of Japanese ceramic sculpture at the Museum of Fine Arts in Houston, Texas. It simply blew me away, and I was determined to visit Japan and explore more of it.

I managed to book a cheap flight to Tokyo, where I found exactly what I was looking for. So, travel and exploration were back in my life again.

Around the middle years of my seventies, there were hints that things were going to change.

Now that I am in my late seventies, the changes are definitely happening. I do not think that anyone can really understand the aging process until it begins to affect them. You may think you know, but until it is happening to your own body, I don't believe it is possible.

I sometimes feel guilty thinking about my mother and how I did not really comprehend what she was going through. Aging is definitely a challenge, and one that some people excel at, while others struggle. Of course, everyone has a different story and set of circumstances; however, much of one's state of mind and behavior depends on cultivating an appropriate attitude.

Yes, it's hard, but it is also fascinating. It's hard to slow down when there are still so many thing you want to do. It's hard to start losing the mobility you have always taken for granted. It's hard not to be as mentally quick as you used to be.

Yet it is exciting to discover new senses emerging as the physical fades and the spiritual and intuitive grow stronger. I feel much more connected to nature and to all kinds of animate and inanimate things. It almost feels as if my surroundings have become animistic. I value life and every living creature in it, be it the tiniest creature, much more. It is strange to be able to connect to a tiny bug.

I also find that minimalizing is becoming a necessity. Changing my usual approach seems to be the key to not feeling overwhelmed. I still read, work in my studio, and travel, but my agendas and expectations have been reduced. There is still much to enjoy, but if you feel overwhelmed, it can become stressful, and you may feel a sense of age.

I am paying much closer attention to my body now and trying to help it adapt as much as possible to the numerous, constant changes taking place. Exercise is a higher priority than ever. 'Just keep moving' is becoming my mantra.

Actually, I love this new side of myself, cultivated through long walks, weightlifting, movement classes, and saunas—a daily consciousness. As a younger woman, I loved to start the day by making a cup of coffee, returning to bed, and reading for at least an hour. Now, I get up and start moving.

These years have given me the time to pursue things that I could never have squeezed into my earlier working years.

I was able to start volunteering at an animal shelter, where I walked and fostered dogs. Being of help to needy animals and forming relationships with them has been incredibly enriching, and I feel very grateful to them for helping me step out of myself. What a relief and what fun! Even with the inevitable heartaches that come with the job, it has been so worthwhile.

It also led my husband and me to our dog, who has become the center point of our lives.

Staying curious and maintaining a passion for learning can be pursued in the seventies, even if one is not very mobile and unable to travel.

The pandemic presented an opportunity to learn Italian, which I had begun in my thirties and then given up as life conditions intruded. Learning a language opens up a new world, which is so exciting and stimulating. You not only exercise your brain, but you also gain a different perspective on things. You keep learning.

Finally, the seventies are a time when one finds oneself the oldest, or nearly so, in a group of people. This has led me to reflect on the importance of being a role model for younger people who have not yet experienced what it is like to grow old.

I do not want to be a miserable, bitter old woman. I want to reflect on my life and what I have learned from it in a positive way: wisdom, laughter, love, sadness, heartache, disappointment, frustration, satisfaction, and fulfillment. This seems to be a goal for the coming years."

Chyrell Botts, Texas, USA.

Chapter Thirteen

Joyce

Going down for a nap

With napping as her favorite activity, Joyce examines the pros and cons of, and social attitudes towards, this age related phenomenon.

"I wanted to write about my new favorite pastime, and I have divided up my essay into two parts.

First, let me say that I love napping and I am not ashamed of it. I wake up from a nap refreshed, physically and mentally, for the rest of my day. Sometimes, I admit, that I wake up a little groggy and don't know where I am for a few seconds, but most of the time, I set the alarm on my phone and snooze happily for thirty to ninety minutes. Every day.

Part One: Resistance. I was in my late sixties when I started to struggle with an overwhelming desire to take a nap in the afternoon. At first, I thought it was because I was eating lunch later, which was triggering afternoon sleepiness, and so I skipped breakfast and ate brunch.

Then I tried going out in the afternoons, making a point of exercising or running an errand to stave off the urge to climb onto any soft surface and close my eyes for thirty minutes. My nocturnal sleeping habits were not good—sometimes I woke up twice a night to visit the bathroom—but I'd addressed this by not drinking any fluids after 8 p.m. So why did I feel like I needed a nap in the afternoon?

My doctor laughed at me—never a good experience to have your concerns laughed at by a doctor—and he just said, 'It's your age. You'll get used to it.'

I asked my friends. One or two confessed that they napped—without guilt—every afternoon. Others denied daily napping but confessed to the occasional afternoon snooze, but only at weekends. *Only at weekends*, I thought, *You haven't worked in a decade; what difference does it make if it's a Saturday or Sunday?*

Still, the afternoon sleepiness persisted. Occasionally, I would allow myself a 'treat' as I thought of it, lying on my sofa, pulling my favorite throw blanket up to my shoulders, snuggling beneath its warmth, resting my hands on my stomach, and closing my eyes.

I did wonder, in this pose, that if someone were to walk in, they might think that I had died in my sleep. I allowed myself to take this nap treat only a few days a week, until it occurred to me that I was rationing myself. *For what and for whom?* I thought.

I continued to struggle with my sleep and nap routines for years. I adjusted the time I went to bed and woke up, counted how many hours I slept, and decided whether to make up those hours with naps during the day. I changed my diet several times—eating sleep inducing foods at night and trying to avoid those during the day—but that didn't work well for me.

Turkey has a reputation for making one sleepy. Still, a turkey snack at night was not appealing to me, and I rather think the sleepiness associated with turkey has more to do with an annual Thanksgiving dinner.

Part Two: Acceptance. By the time I reached seventy-three years of age, napping had become part of the rhythm of my daily life. Wake up, stretch, coffee and breakfast, walk with friends, light lunch, afternoon nap—starting at 2 p.m.—dinner, and bed.

When contemplating visiting my family, I debated telling them, 'Mom/Granny is going to her room for a nap.' What would they think? Their vibrant mother, who seemed to function on the fumes in the air when they were small? Who had boundless energy? A mom who now needs a nap to be able to get through the day?

Friends suggested trips. I worried about my stamina. Would I be able to keep going all day, sightseeing, or would I fall asleep on a tourist bus, slack-mouthed, drooling, or snoring, or perhaps all three? Or on a train? What if I missed my stop because I couldn't stay awake? Or what if my luggage was stolen because I was slumped over in my seat and snoozing?

If we ate a big lunch somewhere, where would I curl up for a nap afterward? I wondered if the need to nap limited the activity and socialization of older people, because I felt it was limiting my social life.

These days, I plan to nap every day, but often lie down and close my eyes for ten or fifteen minutes—well, thirty at most. On other days, I set my alarm and sleep for an hour.

The explanation I found that suited me best—at least this was how I explained napping to myself—and others, was this: 'You don't sleep for eight or nine hours a night, so all you are doing is breaking up your sleep; six or seven hours at night supplemented by an hour or so during the day.' It's working for me.

My grandson commented recently over a family dinner that Granny and his new baby sister had something in common: they both took a lot of naps."

Chapter Fourteen

Kathy (Kelly) Maddocks

Exceeding retirement expectations

A resolute educator, Kathy has worked decades beyond her initial expectations and has yet to set a retirement date. She feels fortunate to have truly loved her work, which has included promotions, increased responsibility, and travel. She will never stop learning and plans to complete her PhD upon her eventual retirement from education.

"It's astonishing to think that in January 2026, I will have been in education for half a century. I am still working, thanks to the UK 2010 Equality Act (age and gender are two of the protected characteristics) and to my own determination and destiny.

My father was a civil servant, and he was forced to retire from the role of principal at sixty and from being a surveyor at sixty-five. Thank goodness, that isn't the case now; I will turn seventy-three in December 2025.

Over the years, since I began teaching in 1976, I have witnessed many changes in education. Graduating with a degree in American Studies, I was assigned to teach geography, English, and art in my first job, despite lacking qualifications to teach art.

As my career developed, I taught English exclusively, and eventually, I was put in charge of the English department of a sixth form (12th and 13th grades). Teaching these students, for me, was always the icing on the cake.

My final role in teaching was as a deputy headteacher in a large school in a more urban area. While I considered myself to be at the 'chalk face' every day for thirty-three years, there wasn't a day that I didn't get a boost from my role. Although there were natural ups and downs and more difficult classes, there were always special moments. No day was the same.

As a teacher, I had envisioned retiring at fifty-five, but, ironically, it was at that age that I took a position that helped me change my attitude. This was in 2009, and I left working in schools to take up a government-sponsored post as a regional advisor on school improvement in the southwest of England.

The post lasted two years, and then I set up my own school improvement company, which kept me busy but left enough time to inspect schools for the UK Office for Standards in Education; I had trained to be an inspector several years previously, when an Inspector (one of Her Majesty's Inspectors—now His Majesty, of course), in the process of inspecting the school I was working in, inspired me to explore this role.

In 2016, at the age of sixty-three, I was asked if I would be interested in becoming an HMI myself. I felt very honored. The roles of HMI were first appointed in 1839, so this is a long tradition in the UK.

My career as an HMI was a wonderful time in my life, expanding my knowledge beyond grade schoolers to understand the learning needs and educational priorities of children in nurseries, pre-school (pre-K), and Reception (Kindergarten). We inspect small independent schools and special schools, as well as inspecting school-centered initial teacher training and education in universities.

As education plays a part in social service care inspections, we also need to understand what is happening to children who are fostered or in children's homes. We team up with Police, Fire, and Rescue Services departments, as well as Health Services, which means I receive an incredible training that enriches the job's rewards. This special training has made me a viable educationalist today.

I am not sure how long I will continue working, but while I feel that I can do some good in this critical sphere, I will continue.

When I stop, I think I will go back to my studies. I began a PhD in 2012 in my original area of interest; for my education degree, my dissertation was on Nathaniel Hawthorne and the impact of Puritanism on his novels. My PhD is on Elizabeth Stuart Phelps Ward, a prolific novelist, poet, journalist, and early feminist, born just after the Civil War into a family of Calvinists. She challenged many Christian beliefs and advocated for reform in women's clothing.

I have been happily married for forty-four years, and I have two wonderful children, but, as yet, there are no grandchildren.

Education has defined my life. I was always happy in school, and I believed that teaching would be my career. But I am not naive, and I recognize that as teachers and educationalists, we must be aware that we are the exception; not everyone loves learning and sharing their knowledge as much as we do. Many people, particularly parents, may not share our views on school and education.

For me, this is the most rewarding thing and something I will never forget; I have always striven to look outwards, to be aware of the circumstances of others and why education may not be their priority, although it has always been mine."

Kathy (Kelly) Maddocks, Somerset, UK

Chapter Fifteen

Susan

What to do with Mom

Feeling as if she had been acting responsibly in arranging her life during her sixties, Susan realized that her plans may have been less than adequate as she approached her middle seventies.

"U nexpectedly laid off from work in my late sixties, I was at first angry and my pride was hurt, but then I became fearful. I had thought I was secure in my job, and in hindsight, I should have paid more attention to the undercurrents at work and read the silent signals.

When I wasn't invited to meetings, I thought I was being given more time to work on projects, but that wasn't the case at all. In retrospect, it was silly of me to feel the way I was thinking, a way that suited me, and perhaps I had just become too comfortable.

The emotional shock was one thing, something I could rationalize, in time, but the financial shock was long-lasting. I had set up my financial structure to work until my seventieth birthday; now I was three years short of retirement contributions and other savings, which I had been steadily increasing each year I worked.

While immediately applying for jobs, I realized that I was not really well-equipped to work elsewhere. I had been working at the same company for twenty years, and during that time I had become well-versed in all their systems and processes. To work somewhere else in a similar position (and with similar pay), I would have to learn new systems.

No one was willing to take a chance on me and let me learn new skills. Do I think age was an issue here? What do you think that answer would be?

I used part of the severance money to take a trip to see an old friend. I called it my 'vengeance tour,' but that was just an excuse. I didn't regret it, although it wasn't a smart move because I spent far too much money.

A widow since my husband died, I was fortunate to have the house paid off with the life insurance money he left, but there wasn't much more, as we'd used up most of our savings in paying for the type of healthcare he'd required for almost a decade.

Upon his death, I had disbursed what was left to our two adult children, despite being advised not to do so and to keep the money as part of my estate. I wanted to give the children something to remember him by.

pleasant, friendly, and seemingly understanding, I thought I heard judgment in every word he spoke and did not respond to his requests. I am sure I was being oversensitive, but I couldn't help my feelings. On reflection, he could have helped me.

Selling my house was an option, and I could have bought something smaller, but then where would my children and grandchildren stay when they came to town? If I had a smaller home, perhaps without offering them somewhere to stay, they might not visit at all.

I started chipping away at my expenses, sticking to a monthly budget based on my pension and avoiding dipping into my savings. I am sure that the profound anxiety I had around money contributed to my mental health and then my physical health, and by the time I was seventy-two I was in poor physical shape.

Depression had removed any thought of exercise and activity, and I had become over-weight and familiar with many of the pesky ailments that are associated with age. By seventy-four, I realized that if I were going to live another decade, I would be doing so in poor health, as I couldn't find it within myself to become motivated.

A fall, a broken bone, an extended stay in the hospital during which time I contracted pneumonia, and I realized that living alone may no longer be an option for me.

I turned to my children, got them both on the phone at the same time—without their spouses, though they may have been listening—and told them that I needed to make plans for my long-term care. My son asked me if I had any long-term care insurance (I didn't), and my daughter asked how much longer I thought I could manage alone (I didn't know for sure).

There were long silences on the phone. I heard a TV in the background of one house, and children playing, calling to each other in the yard of the other house, and I realized that this phone call would now upend many lives. What to do with Mom?

The silence on the phone was so long that I suggested we speak again at another time. My daughter asked before we hung up, 'What does this actually, mean, Mom, for us, for me and my kids, my family?' My son was silent. Then, he said, 'You know we'll have to tell our spouses about this, because it will involve all of us.'

My humiliation hit an all time low. Now my daughter-in-law and my son-in-law would know the extent of my financial mismanagement. Would they ever look at me the same way again? How would I rob them of their lives? Would they resent me?

My children said they would talk it over and then get back to me. I've had to make three terrible phone calls in my life, one to each child to let them know their father had passed, and now this one. The first two calls were expected; this one was a shock to the recipients.

As I write this, I am waiting for my son to arrive at my house, the task having been designated to him by his sister, no doubt taking a day off work because his weekends are packed with child-related activities. Together, we are planning to go through all my finances.

In the last decade, I have become a version of myself that I would not have recognized in earlier decades. Where I once felt vibrant, I now feel tepid, lukewarm, pale, and uninteresting. I guess that one or the other of the children will offer to have me live near them so they can keep an eye on me, but I wish I didn't have to ask this.

My children do not live near each other, which likely means I will see less of one family and more of the other. I wonder how they will draw that straw?

It will be suggested, more like recommended, that I sell the house, buy something smaller—a ground floor apartment—and use the rest of the money to live on. I won't be able to drive, as my eyesight is just one of my many challenges, so the car needs to be sold as well.

Helping my children on a practical level seems out of the question. My ailments make chasing small children a challenge. Maybe I can help around the house with the dishes, although I often feel shooed out of the way as I interrupt routines and ask too many questions about what belongs where.

I can't bend easily or get up off the floor to help with the youngest grandchildren. I am not trusted enough to spend time alone with them unless we are all engaged in sedentary pursuits, indoors. I do think I will be able to help the grandchildren with their homework, and perhaps other neighborhood children as well.

No one wants this. There are other people involved, also. My son-and daughter-in-law each have sets of parents living. Although people will be friendly and say, 'That's great that your mom is moving closer to be with you,' that sentence whitewashes a lot of emotions and disguises the many circumstances that led up to this.

My friends will tell me I'm lucky, as they are also in their seventies and some are in their eighties, awaiting their fate, but I will lose these friendships as I move far away.

I am trying to look on the bright side of all of this. Feeling pity and sorry for myself is not how I want to present myself to anyone, so every morning I give myself a good talking-to, trying to remain optimistic and uncomplaining, in approaching something that I never wanted. I know my children and grandchildren love me, and feeling their love is really what is carrying me through all of this change."

Meg

"If you spend any time online or talking to friends you will read and hear about women in their sixties and seventies who are embarking on new journeys. A relationship, broken, fractured, and finalized in an attorney's office, has created a gap in the continuity of many lives, and now each woman is striking out in a new direction, documenting her experiences in many cases. This is new. And I think it's good, because these pioneering women will give hope and reassurance to others."

Wendy

"Sometimes I wonder if I'm too late. In my sixties I let myself go, particularly my physical health as a result of my poor mental health, and the journey back to mental and physical health is a long once, but I am determined to get there. I am motivated by the examples I see around me of women in their seventies who are living great lives. I want to live my own great life—before it's late."

Chapter Sixteen

Linda Cahan

Pursuing love in many places

After giving and receiving love for many years, Linda finally realized that loving someone and being in a partnership are essential parts of her identity and will be for the rest of her life. She just never thought that she'd be single—again—and in her seventies, with a body that wasn't what it once was.

"Like many of my friends, I got married right out of college in 1971, which was not a great idea, and I rectified it by leaving my husband in 1983. I thought that I'd remarry fairly quickly but, instead, I was single for sixteen long years.

In my search for true love during those years, I was Rolfed, kneaded, 'shiatsued,' 'watsued,' healed, peeled, 'Reikied,' crystal-cleansed, analyzed, computerized, bio-energized, Jung-ed, 'Freuded,' 'Rilked,' and bilked. The amount of money I spent on psychic readings, alone, invested wisely, would today have made a valid retirement fund.

But after sixteen years of intensive hoping, dreaming, scheming, manifesting, praying, and trying, I finally found my true love. The bliss and deep joy this brought me changed me and my life. Then, after twenty-two years of contented love, he died, and at seventy-one years old, I started the process all over again.

My slightly younger husband died of lung cancer, four months after being diagnosed. He chose to take his life thanks to the *Death with Dignity* law in Oregon, which is a true blessing. He was diagnosed in September and died right after Christmas in 2020.

At seventy-one, I joined the 'widow's club,' and during those four months after my husband's diagnosis, I had to figure out what to do with my immediate future. Within the first three months, I had traded in both Subarus for a new model, had two estate sales, donated thirty-six bags of clothing to shelters, house-hunted for a much smaller home, put my home on the market, sold it overnight, and bought a new, smaller place the next day.

It was a whirlwind, and I never stopped—until I tripped over the door jamb to my new house while multitasking and broke my arm ten days before moving day. Thanks to my sister and great friends who packed me up and unpacked me, I was able to make the move. But I still didn't slow down; it was my coping mechanism.

I never thought I'd be single in my seventies. This time I skipped all the treatments that had helped me feel ready to accept love before. After giving and receiving love for so many years, I finally realized that being in a relationship is an essential part of who I am, and who I will be for the rest of my life.

Of course, at seventy-one, my body wasn't what it once was; it wasn't even particularly great at fifty-one when I got married. I wish I could take back most of the money I spent on various weird shit and put it toward a facelift and liposuction, but in the immortal words of Popeye—'I y'am what I y'am.' And it's not so bad.

So I ventured online to see if anyone was interested in me and me in them. I'm a redhead, and some men are attracted to us as a sub-species. Ask most redheads how they feel about the statement 'I'm really into redheads,' and you'll know that most men who say that do not actually get into a redhead. It makes us feel less like a person and more like a hobby or a collector's item.

I met some very nice men—truly. The horror stories I'd heard from friends did not happen to me. One dear, beautiful friend fell in love with a man who was oddly unavailable at crucial times during the two years they dated. He always had good reasons for his absences, but it started to feel fishy.

As it turned out, it was beyond fishy. Just as they were jointly planning for him to move into her home, two women rang her doorbell. She was deeply shocked to find out that this love of hers was also steadily seeing these two women, as well as three other women! He was juggling six women and professing love to each of them.

I do believe that he was convinced that what he was saying and feeling was true, but he was a sick puppy. I'd love to use another word for 'puppy,' but I'll let you fill that in. My friend was, and still is, devastated; her trust in men and in her instincts are shattered.

My friend's experience had me on high alert. I have good instincts, but I've been fooled a few times. Committing to love is like adopting a pet—it's a lifelong commitment for me. That's what made it so difficult to leave my first husband, but when he was mean, he was very, very mean. So, with lessons learned, I went to each new date with my eyes open and my heart wary.

I was love-bombed by a smart, funny, seemingly great guy whom I quickly fell for. I hadn't had sex for over two and a half years and I was so ready! He claimed the same, and I believed him. After twenty-two years of 'married' sex—where it works well but gets more than a bit routine, this guy wanted to do it all—for hours. Not that I got bored, but I was put off by certain things that I'd never enjoyed and didn't want to try again.

I was finally old enough and sure enough of myself to say 'no' to some things and be interested in trying others. It was late summer when he knelt down to lick my toes—that was a major 'NO!' I am insanely ticklish, and I was afraid that I'd kick him in the nose. Plus, it's not as if I'd had the chance to wash my feet first. While some people may think, *she doesn't know what she missed,* yes I do, and I don't care.

Bottom line, he called to tell me that he was dealing with some family issues and would be out of touch for a while. He declined my offers of help, and then, after sending me many daily texts and seeing me frequently, he disappeared.

After weighing things up, my intuition kicked in, and two weeks later I texted him and asked if he'd prefer to break up. 'Definitely not!' was his answer, so I hung in and wondered when the family issues would be resolved. I never heard from him again.

Later, I realized that he'd met someone else and that he didn't have the courage to tell me. All I needed was honesty and clarity, and I could have let go easily; I'm well aware that if it's not working for one of a pair, it's not working at all.

I went back online and had many one-time-only dates. Sometimes, it was an instant 'no' when I met someone; other times, we would talk longer, and I'd still feel that something was off. Some men weren't attracted to me, and that was okay, too. Meeting the right person takes persistence and an enormous amount of luck.

Once, I was on what started as a nice date. Two hours into our conversation, he asked me about my 'dealbreak-ers.' I'd never been asked that before and replied, 'A lack of honesty and integrity, meanness and irresponsibility.' He nodded and launched into a story about how he had put on a shoe, while sockless, and discovered that his pet cat had shit in his shoe. He cleaned off his foot, put the cat in a box, and took it to the local shelter.

The woman at the shelter questioned him about bringing in the cat for one infraction, pointing out that cat must have been very upset about something and was communicating to him. But he took it as an unforgivable insult and left the cat to its fate. That was a dealbreaker for me. It took two hours to learn that I could never respect or trust this man.

I was ready to give up online dating. I told my sister, who is a psychologist, and she firmly encouraged me to keep trying and not to give up. I had a few more dates that didn't pan out and then one that did—in a big way!

When this man walked up to the table at the restaurant, something kind of 'pinged' in me, it was a sense of recognition, but I didn't know why. Our conversation was easy, and we had some fun things in common. I really liked the TV show *Young Sheldon,* a sitcom with depth and humor. It was also one of his favorites, and I was stunned. I had kept meeting men who not only looked down on TV but who wouldn't have given that show a first look, assuming it would be idiotic.

This man was also exceptionally well-educated and equally funny. Also, he appeared to be highly responsible, which is important to me. We agreed to meet for a second date at a dive bar near his place. It was an odd choice for a second date, but I'm always open to trying new places, especially if they offer good burgers. Sadly, the burger was not great, but we had another interesting conversation.

When we left, I saw his van, which had no side windows. It looked to me like a serial killer's ride, and I was shocked. That night, I became very anxious. It's not as if I knew his friends or family—he was just some random guy I'd met who drove a creepy-looking van.

My instincts told me that he was a good man, but my anxiety kept me from sleeping. Somehow, I got past my fear and asked him why he was driving a windowless van. His goal had been to outfit it for camping and fishing. *Oh, much less anxiety.* For our fourth date he was driving a very non-serial killer Scion sportscar. He'd heard my anxiety and decided to get a better ride.

The van wasn't a deal breaker for me, but it wasn't an attraction. His response was excellent and deeply appreciated. We have been together for over a year now. Neither of us want to remarry or live together, we enjoy our visits and vacations, and our time apart. We exchanged 'I love you's' about six months into our relationship. I have said those words to very, very few men. When I told my close friend about this breakthrough, she asked, 'So what's the next step?'

There is no next step. I'm committed, as is he. He's my emergency contact, and he was there for me when I needed him. I'll be there for him. Our cats will never meet! We both have two male cats; it wouldn't be pretty.

As with many women, my lust had waned after menopause. But it didn't go away completely, and I still have desire—just not as often. Luckily, my guy was up for it—so to speak. There was only one problem, and it was mine, not his; every time we had sex, I'd end up at the chiropractor or acupuncturist. I kept pulling something or hurting myself, and it's not like we were doing any weird Kama Sutra positions. I'm just seventy-six years old.

My body has become cranky and is annoyed by certain positions that used to feel very satisfying. It wasn't only embarrassing but expensive, because my acupuncturist doesn't take Medicare. My guy didn't want me to be uncomfortable or in pain, so we started experimenting, which is fun.

Older bodies can be responsive, especially if one's partner is willing. I've finally learned to communicate and luckily found a man who listens and responds to me. I also discovered a lubricant that works for me, so having sex doesn't feel as if I'm being 'de-virginized' each time, bringing back much-needed elasticity to what had turned into a Sahara.

When I look in the mirror I don't see age, I see me—Linda—not an 'old lady.' My essence is as vital as ever. I may get tired more quickly and take afternoon naps sometimes, after meditation, but I can become like a six-year-old when I see a butterfly, and I feel deep joy listening to my cat purr.

People who say it's impossible to find love after a certain age will probably create their own reality, believing this to be true. What you focus on grows. I believed I would find love again, and I am so grateful that I did. And I am really picky; I don't settle. What matters is that I know how to compromise without losing myself. Being in my seventies and having accrued wisdom and self-confidence over time helps! I also believe in prayer and luck."

Linda Cahan, Oregon, USA

———⋙⋘———

Catherine

"There are four words I am living by in my seventies: 'action' (staying fit), 'accountability' (being honest with myself), 'audacity' (being brave but not reckless), and 'amazing' (I want to be amazing)."

———⋙⋘———

Mary Ellen

"In my fifties, I had no interest in women who discussed their favorite ice cream flavors—their not-so-secret pleasures to finish an evening meal or snack just before turning in for the night. At the time, I was worried about my weight and the impact of extra calories. In my sixties, I became curious—or maybe latent sweet cravings were kicking in—and started adding ice cream containers to my shopping cart.

In my seventies, I found myself comparing notes with other women about our favorite flavors and brands. I remembered conversations I'd shared with friends in my teens about which movie star was 'hot' or not, whose looks we liked and why—although we all went on to date and marry men who didn't look anything like our movie crushes. Now, in our seventies, talking about ice cream flavors is so much more satisfying."

Chapter Seventeen

Jeri Kadison

Self-care is not self-indulgence

At seventy-eight, Jeri finally understood that you cannot change anyone else. She now recognizes that the changes she desired in others must first come from herself. After decades, this realization has improved her relationships with her children and their spouses, albeit later in life. She believes it's never too late.

"Since turning seventy, which happened in 2017, time has whizzed by. I know I am not alone in feeling this way. I would love it if time could slow down, and although I've asked Father Time to slow time down—of course, I know that's not possible—I finally answered the question for myself: in my mind, and it is in my mind, I can slow down time.

For years, I have squandered time, wallowing in remorse and regret—as if either sentiment could change the past. But, finally, at seventy-three years of age, I walked through the doors of a twelve-step program for the friends and family of people who are affected by addiction. At Nar-Anon, I learned to stop trying to rescue everyone else, to stop trying to earn love from people who had none to give, especially a mother who was never going to be kind and had certainly never protected me. Over time, I learned to rescue myself.

Recovery revealed the truth behind years of pain, from childhood abuse, domestic violence, and financial betrayal. I have taken on the shame of my abusers for far too long.

At this point, I have taken my life back with dignity. My children tell me that they are proud of who I've become, and at seventy-eight, I'm thriving.

While I've always been resilient, for far too long I got up only to walk the same path, repeating the same steps, but that's not healing. Healing required something new of me, new actions, new tools, and finding a new path.

My recovery has taught me to set boundaries, to communicate with compassion, to pause before reacting, and to stop giving my power away to people who never deserved it. It's also taught me to ask for help, without shame, because few of us can live through difficult times alone. I have made amends, I've forgiven, and I have been forgiven. I've finally learned that self-care is not self-indulgence.

My seventies have lit up my soul again—I'm back to doing what fills me with joy. I feel fortunate that I love my work. I've spent my career as an Integrative Medicine Coach and Language and Speech Pathologist, helping others to find their voices. Finally, I have my voice, and I am practicing what I studied and now teach.

My passion for my work and the need to recover and establish a financial foundation—after mine was taken from me—is my reason to move forward, and I am doing so with a sparkle and a zest for life that includes travel. I am also open to allowing a good man into my life.

I've also learned to turn curses into blessings. That includes physical challenges, including two total knee replacements. Receiving help is as rewarding as giving it, and I have needed help on a practical level.

As to slowing down time, the answer has been mindfulness all along. The same mindfulness I once taught others in a hospital setting is now a practice I return to every day, breathing, pausing, praying, and staying in the moment. I really understand what it means to treasure every moment and not to dwell on regrets and wishes, but to make new memories knowing that I deserve them.

I will continue to write, sing, and work, and I will keep showing up for others as well as myself. When I meet roadblocks, I will view them not as obstacles, but as stepping stones."

Jeri Kadison, New Jersey, USA.

Brenda

"I can't be the only one—I know I am not the only one, a solo traveler during the last decades of my life. I've always been such a people person, surrounding myself with family, friends, and acquaintances, always the outgoing, gregarious, life and soul of a party. But now I crave my own company more than I want to be around other people.

If you had asked me years ago if I could spend days alone, I would have hesitated before answering, but not today, when sometimes, I feel rudely interrupted from my reverie when the phone rings. I am not yet talking to myself, maybe that's not far off—but as long as I am happy and not bothering anyone else, does it matter?"

Chapter Eighteen

Carol Jean Bradford

Wanting to be old

Not everyone desires to age, but Carol has always wanted to be older than her years, eager for each decade. The years provide increasing clarity to the past and optimism for the future in the time that's still available.

"Since I can remember, I've always wanted to be old. Well, I made it. I'm seventy-six, but I still think eighty-six will be better. I've reached a point in my life where I can finally make any decision I want, not one I have to make. A time when I choose to have a quiet glass of wine alone and reflect. A time that, in running this race, I know that finishing first, second, or even third does not mean as much to me, only that I am going to finish in the place of my choosing. I appreciate all the hurdles jumped, puddles stepped in, and falls taken, because I've learned to get up and get going.

Being born mid-century, I've seen lots of changes and progress, some good and some not so good. I still take my mother's advice and heed my father's warnings, though I walk my own paths.

I've lost and won at love. I've experienced unbearable loss and found that I would survive. I'm a single mom of three beautiful children, a grandmother to eight granddaughters, and a great-grandmother to seven boys and three girls. It gives me pleasure to sit and listen to their chatter about life, because I know they will make it. They come from strong stock.

I once heard the term 'to endeavor to persevere,' and it stuck with me. This term has carried me through ups and downs. I guess that if I have anything to pass along it would be that all things happen for a reason. You just have to be faithful and patient enough to weather the storms that come your way. Be open and understanding, because knowledge can come from the oldest or the youngest in the room. In the end, it pays to be fair and considerate.

I've been afforded the opportunity to have dinner and dance with my favorite President and his wife. I have been on tour with my favorite hip hop artist. I maintain a handful of good friends, three of whom I've known for over fifty years.

A very good life includes challenges. I've tried to recognize my weaknesses, build on my strengths, and rely on my wit to help me along. I learned this from my grandmother, who could neither read nor write but became a landowner and a prosperous, valued member of her community.

Today, at seventy-six, I'm starting a new business that I plan, along with my partners, to build into a multi-billion dollar enterprise. Here I go! Off into the world."

Carol Jean Bradford, Texas, USA.

Janet

"Not a naturally active person, I force myself to keep moving in my seventies. Movement is the key to everything. In my head, I keep a vision of an elderly person sitting in a chair most of the day because either they can't—or won't—move. That's a warning vision of someone I do not want to be.

If one is disabled in some way and movement is impossible, I understand, but everyone else owes it to themselves, their bodies, and their minds—and their families, who might have to take care of them—to keep moving.

Move every hour. You'd be surprised at how many hours can pass when all you're doing is looking at a TV screen. I find reasons to get up and move about, even though I don't want to. I try to take the stairs even when I feel like everything is slowing down and it's painful.

In the past, I used to bundle everything together at the foot of the stairs and take it all upstairs in a basket, but now I force myself to make three trips, whereas before I would have made one. I've started to find things to do to keep moving. Nothing good comes from sitting in a chair for hours.

People assume that I'll want to live in a one-story house one day, but they must have a different vision of me. I suppose it's inevitable—not so much the climb up the stairs as the risk of falling when coming downstairs.

While I agree constant movement increases the risks of a fall, the day I stop challenging myself physically will be the first day of my physical decline."

———❦———

Cath

"Why do I hike? Why do I enjoy climbing mountains? Why am I focused on accomplishing physical feats? For this one simple reason: because at seventy-three, I still can. I am proud of my ability to keep pushing myself. I'll choose the moment I think of myself as an 'old lady'; that's not up to anyone else."

———❦———

Chapter Nineteen

Louella

We aren't friends anymore

Pinky swear friends for life. That's how it always was between Louella and her best friend—until it wasn't, until she became someone Louella no longer recognized. But had the friend changed, or had Louella?

"We had been the best of friends since college, immediately forging a friendship when a lottery placed us together in a dorm room. Our friendship was sustained over our twenties as we launched ourselves into the world, in our thirties as we married and had children, sharing stories of the struggles of parenting and managing cooperative or not-so-cooperative husbands.

We remained steadfast and determined friends in our forties—not easy when you live at opposite ends of the country—even after I divorced and embarked on a new life that at the time seemed unrecognizable, almost shocking, to my friend.

In our fifties, while I was exploring dating, she abruptly left her husband, her life, and moved to another state and never provided an explanation for her actions, except that she needed to do something for herself. I thought it might be menopause, but she claims she never really experienced menopause.

Perhaps she couldn't explain her actions. I didn't judge her for the spur-of-the moment action, although clearly there was some planning behind it, conscious or unconscious; she needed to get away, but she literally ran away—not from a life-threatening situation. I think she ran away from herself.

To this day, I don't know why she did that. I think she has told herself many stories as to why she abruptly changed her life, but I have not heard any of them.

Many of us have made swift moves to extricate ourselves from situations we were incapable of understanding at the time, situations that did not feed our needs, situations that we may have found threatening, situations that were no longer sustainable, and the reasons we provided to ourselves—and others—that may have held up over time, or maybe over the same amount of time, they now sound feeble and inadequate, and so we keep quiet. Or provide another explanation.

It's not for me to judge, but I do, or at least I question. It takes courage to make radical change, but there's a flip side:

a sense of accountability that one day you may—mostly likely will—have to confront.

I'm not religious, but I think there is some day of judgment when you have to come to terms with your actions, or the thoughts gnaw away at you, until you either let them destroy you—because it's a choice to acknowledge them—or you face them and come to terms with the consequences. 'This is what I did. This is who I was at the time.'

Fast-forward to now. We are both in our seventies. I am seventy-one and she is seventy-two, and we couldn't be farther apart—physically, emotionally, geographically.

I remarried, eventually, to a man who is younger than I am, and I find this refreshing—although all marriages are challenging—because he does not have the same expectations of me as a man of my generation (or older). Our marriage is interesting and unconventional, and it is working beyond my expectations, given that I always thought he would leave me for someone younger.

My friend remarried a much older man. Their world is run according to his needs and expectations, especially in the areas of diet, healthcare, and social life. She just fills in around him with various hobbies and activities, but she is always part of the satellite of being a 'couple,' which, I understand, is very important to her at this stage in life. His friends, most of whom she has nothing in common with, and his family, who don't seem to care for her, although

Our daughter put the money to good use, toward renovating her home, but I am not sure what my son did with the money; I remind my self that it isn't any of my business.

So there I was, sixty-seven and without a job. I qualified for Social Security, but my retirement savings were small. I attended a free tax seminar and was shocked by just how poorly my husband and I had planned. Or, put another way, had failed to plan. The speaker rattled on about long-term care, insurance, and savings. As I listened, I grew increasingly distressed.

All the questions I had of the speaker stuck in my throat. I listened as others bravely outlined their financial circumstances. Still, many of the questions seemed to focus on the taxation of assets and complicated financial circumstances that did not apply to me.

On the way to the car park in the cool, chill evening of a fall night, I vowed to immediately reduce all my expenses. I felt that I had no one to talk to. I didn't want to confide in my children because I would feel ashamed, not only of the example I would be setting but also of my poor financial management. It wasn't the sort of thing that you talked to friends about.

At one point, I contacted a financial planner, but he insisted on seeing every expense I'd made over the last two years, every expense I could anticipate over the next year, and every subsequent year. The scrutiny amplified my feelings of inadequacy and incompetence. Although he was during my difficult times—although it took her a while to understand that my view of happiness was not the same as hers—but I deeply appreciated her for her constancy and her attempts to understand me.

Or did I get lost? I don't think of myself as lost. Or did our relationship get lost? Today, I ask myself how we, as two women who had so much in common over the decades, are now at some sort of stand off. How are we so 'unalike' when we started out in a place of commonality?

In a marriage, particularly a lop-sided one, I understand how differences in values or outlook can widen cracks that already existed between those inside the marriage, or even pinpoint cracks that are emerging, but friendship with your best friend? How did I get that so wrong?

There are things she says today that remind me of my mother's generation. She doesn't 'approve' of this, that, or the other, although these are things that are time proven, so it is just her opinion. These comments make her appear outdated. I think the voice I hear is actually her husband's voice.

My friend has decided that the 'modern world' as she describes it, is not for her. She wants no part of the digital world that is happening around us, that cannot be denied. She is saying that at seventy-two years old, she is going to avoid anything she doesn't understand or approve of, and she may live to be ninety-one with the same perspective.

In this aspect she reminds me of my grandmother, who wanted no part of a world she did not recognize. Shuttered, closed off, yet still expectant that people would view the world through her lens.

If we both live to be in our eighties I anticipate our conversations to be increasingly truncated and formulaic, with us respectfully asking about each others families, etc., but that bond of connection is now a thin string of familiarity that neither of us wants to cut.

Let's face it, friends are disappearing every year, swallowed up willingly or not, into lives they may or may not have planned, and then some friends have died. So, we cling to the strands, the threads of history, to remind us of who we are.

But how does this really serve either of us? Are we just not willing to say, 'We had a great time—you and I—as friends, and I appreciate your role in my life—but now, when I hear you, I am just saddened, disappointed (well, that's on me for wanting more for you than you want for yourself), and ultimately, quiet, because perhaps, after all, there is nothing left to say?"

Chapter Twenty

Constance Soutullo

Living life with optimism

Having a vast appetite for living, Constance embraces life with creativity and curiosity, greeting each day by kissing her life "'hello."

"Left-handed and born under the sign of Aquarius, I've never held traditional aspirations about life and where it might lead me. I suppose it was written in the stars that I would be a free spirt. I always felt the world was my oyster and fully expected to have an exciting, travel-filled, exotic life. By nature, I am an intuitive risk taker.

As a child, I was endlessly curious, propelled by an inner vision of excitement and glee towards the world. As a young adult in the 1970s, the world was in the midst of explosive radical change, becoming a psychedelic era of art and culture, a swirling cacophony of visual delights. My twenties felt like an off-Broadway play.

Then life offered me a profound experience, one that I had always known would come my way. At the age of thirty-two, I found love while living in New Orleans. We met on a park bench during a Mardi Gras parade at the 1984 World's Fair.

I married a magnificent partner. We were both flexible about having children. Optimism came naturally to us as a couple. We felt like if children came into our marriage, that would be wonderful and if they didn't, we would still be at peace.

But life had its own design. I became a mom at thirty-seven and a half years old to our first daughter. Little did I know how my world would be so beautifully transformed into the highest heights I could have ever imagined.

Curious, because I never really aspired to be a mother, I thought that children would slow me down. Yet life with my firstborn was profound. She entered the world with innate civility and harmony, prodigious from the beginning. I was crazy in love with her.

At forty-two, without fertility problems, we welcomed the birth of our second daughter. Interestingly, both of my babies' names were revealed to me before they were born; one was whispered years earlier as I walked down a street, and the other appeared in a dream.

Our second daughter announced herself with a mellow, magnetic charm and a swagger that made us laugh. 'Grace' was the name we chose for her middle name to honor her arrival. My adjective for her was 'delicious.'

In 1994, at forty-two, with a baby, I had no peers. No one around me was breastfeeding a baby until she was fifteen months old. But it didn't matter. I found my most authentic voice in mothering and trusted what I wanted for our family.

We built a beautiful family nucleus. I immersed myself in our family one thousand percent. I knew these precious souls, my children, were empty vessels, and that what I poured into them would shape them. As an inspired mom, this was a never-ending delight of magic.

When our daughters became teenagers, we wanted them to become global citizens, so we took them on a two-week trip across Europe. Everyone chose their own city. That trip alone holds a book waiting to be written.

If you ask me where my deepest satisfaction lies, I will say, without pause, 'Being a mother to my two daughters.' That journey carried me beyond the universe. But life shifted again. In my early sixties, my husband and I decided to divorce. It felt like, to me, at that time, people rarely spoke of ending a marriage after thirty-plus years, and I had no peers, again, to reflect on.

Although I was advised against it, I knew in my heart that we were not thriving, despite the considerable dedication invested in our union. I made the boldest, bravest choice one could make: to go it alone. My marriage of three decades ended, and with it came the collapse of the life I thought I'd built forever.

No one steps into marriage at a later age believing it will unravel after thirty years, yet there I was—left to face a future that no longer resembled the past. I didn't just lose a partner; I lost the framework of family, familiarity, and stability that I thought would always be mine.

But I believed in the integrity of my soul. Staying together would have meant consigning and resigning, and I could not accept the quiet diminishment that I see too often in older marriages around me.

It took seven years to make the separation viable and years more to rebuild our relationship and keep our family intact, even though we were no longer together. That work was its own kind of marriage. As a result, we continue to support one another and celebrate holidays together as a family.

To reinvent your life in your late sixties, alone, takes grit, courage, confidence, and conviction. I won't pretend otherwise. I never imagined my story would be defined by resilience, but resilience has a way of shaping you quietly, long before you recognize it as your companion. And there's pride, too.

At seventy years old, I bought my own home. I'm still fully employed. My health is excellent, and my curiosity remains endless.

And now, I find that my heart is ready for love again. My daughters are my sounding boards, offering reason, admiration, and infinite love. They are beautifully hearted women. Being an older mother with daughters in their thirties gives me such a fresh perspective on staying in touch with the pulse of younger generations. It's my own alchemy for staying young.

Now, at seventy-three, my pulse quickens with possibility. Life feels like a series of open doors, each one waiting to be flung wide open. I move fast—too fast for some, perhaps—yet this decade has gifted me urgency and joy in equal measure. I write, I imagine, I create.

I want to say 'yes' to everything! My mind is a whirlwind of projects, dreams, and ideas that refuse to be shelved. I also look forward to becoming a grandmother.

I've been on Instagram since 2013, when it was a small community primarily of photographers. This wonderful world ignited my artistic endeavors and feels even richer, connecting me with people and ideas across the globe. Due to this dynamic influence, I am working on a book about navigating life as a solo older woman. Social media has morphed into something slippery, hard to catch, but my resolute friendships are everlasting.

Through all the twists and turns, an inner blossom continues to unfold within me, and I am alive with curiosity and gratitude. I am a Creative. Always, at the core. I came into this life with a vast appetite for living. I've been humbled and challenged by life, but still, I persist.

I will always see the world as my canvas, excited for the beginning of the next brushstrokes in my cherished life, life that I continue to kiss 'hello,' again and again."

Constance Soutullo, Florida, USA.

Peggy

"Late in my sixties, once I'd retired, I tried several different activities, trying to find something to fill up my time. Nothing really worked for me until a friend encouraged me to go to a pottery class. At first, I didn't care for the idea of getting messy but now I love it! I can't wait to get my hands on the clay every morning.

After paying for a few private lessons, I have turned the garage into my pottery studio. We never park the car there, so it seemed the obvious place to make a mess. I've added shelves and now these are lined with my creations. My husband looks on with tolerance. My friends are amused. I am learning, and my pots and vases are starting to look less like misshapen blobs. I've earned this time, my time to find something that I love, and I couldn't be happier."

Chapter Twenty-One

Angela L. Hoy

Completed but never finished

Looking forward to a new decade and the publication of her first book, Angela did not expect the shockwaves that marked the year she turned seventy. While she cannot know what the rest of the year—or decade—may entail, as a two-time cancer survivor, she's firmly tied to each day.

"Early in December of 2024, I stopped working on my new book, a memoir, because my beloved father was admitted to the hospital a couple of days before his ninety-sixth birthday. Our family rushed to his bedside from different cities, believing and hoping he would rally as he'd done multiple times before.

My sister and I arrived with our husbands, joining Dad's wife—our stepmom—and followed by my brother-in-law's sister and husband. We soon realized that Dad was very ill, and we maintained a family presence by his bed day and night.

We poured our love into his tall but frail form, watching him slip into a light coma as we tried to accept what was happening. The hospital was packed with patients, and there were no private rooms to house our grief; Dad shared a room with three other patients. We pulled the curtains and sat in a circle around his bed, sorrowing for our family's cherished patriarch.

A patient in the bed across from Dad was delirious and intermittently yelled out that he was going to make it, then the nurses would dash in and shush her.

The second evening, my sister stayed by his side, waiting to softly sing 'Happy Birthday' to him at midnight. The next morning, a semi-private room opened up, and Dad was moved. More and more, he struggled to breathe and, just a day later, Dad flew into the stars, trailed by broken bits of our hearts.

The rest of December was muted, gray, and forlorn. Dad had been my biggest champion for my book; I deeply missed his presence and our weekly phone chats. My book recounted how my sister and I had been stolen from Dad when we were little girls and survived abuse, neglect, and abandonment. We'd been told he was dead, but as adults, we went on a quest to find him, unraveling mysteries along the way.

In January 2025, I decided to keep heading toward publication—it was the best way I knew to honor my father. Later that month, we traveled to Florida to spend time with my husband's siblings, and I experienced the magic of Sanibel Island for the first time.

The year before our arrival, Hurricanes Milton and Helene had blasted all of the island's famous seashells and most of the sand and beachside structures. Yet by the time of our visit, truckloads of sand had rebuilt the beach, and the shells were returning along with shorebirds and other marine life, including dolphins, just offshore. I marveled at the sea's ability to repair and restore while I wandered, gathering shells for my collection.

On another day, when we drove around to nearby Fort Myers Beach, we were astonished at the remaining damage, and I recalled the absolute devastation we'd observed during our first visit in early 2023. The previous year, Hurricane Ian had smashed buildings and tossed around hundreds of boats that had landed on houses, in yards, swamps, roads, and every other place a boat should not be.

In late February 2025, I entered my seventy-first year. I thought about the storm of loss that had surged through my recent days, and I was grateful that my little ship of life was still sailing.

In March, we landed in Tucson, Arizona, to house-sit for a friend and attend the Tucson Festival of Books. We explored to our hearts' content, including the intriguing and unconventional De Grazia Gallery in the Sun, and connected with friends who were also traveling in the area.

Then, during our final few days, we raced around the book festival to hear as many authors as possible.

My heart expanded and mended a bit more. The day after we got home, in mid-March, I went for my annual mammogram, feeling good about being twenty-seven years past my breast cancer diagnosis. Once I'd reached the quarter century mark, in 2023, without another episode, I'd been claiming my survivor status with more certainty.

A week later, I received a notice to return to the breast center for more imaging. I'd been through this exercise a couple of years earlier and expected the same result. No cancer. Unhappily, the earliest I could schedule the return visit was a month out. There was nothing to do but wait.

The day came, and I went through the diagnostic mammogram and, with my husband nearby, an ultrasound. The doctor then arrived and performed a slow, careful scan of the area the technician had identified. The hum and tick of every machine in the room became amplified as he quietly stared at the ultrasound screen.

Finally, he said, 'Would you like to know what I think?' This was different from the last time I underwent additional screening. 'Yes,' I immediately replied, before I could stop myself. In my mind I was saying, *No, no, no please not again!* He continued, 'I'm ninety-five percent sure it is cancer, the kind that moves at a glacial pace.'

I didn't want that answer, but it was mine. The doctor went on to say that lab analysis would confirm his conclusion, which would take about five to seven days. My brain stopped receiving the continuous flow of information and supportive words.

The clinicians left so I could dress, and my husband came over and grasped my hand. I looked into his worried eyes, and one tear suddenly floated down my cheek.

We went home to wait. The lab analysis confirmed cancer, and our days orbited around medical appointments. Appointments with a surgeon. A call from the surgery scheduler. Messaging with my rheumatologist. Scheduling with oncology. A lengthy discussion with the genetic counselor after I learned that I carry the CHEK2 mutation, giving me a greater chance of developing several types of cancer. A video consultation with the radiologist. Then, we booked the hotel where we'd stay to prepare for my lumpectomy.

Every clinician we encountered was kind, informative, and encouraging. I heard them say things like, 'Stage one, with no spread into lymph nodes, is very good,' The tumor was tiny. Although it was estimated at four millimeters, it turned out to be six millimeters, which is less than a quarter of an inch.

I know from my initial cancer experience that numbers and measurements tie you to, or loosen you from, your life. The first time, the tumor was more than an inch, leaving me with a poor prognosis. Back then, several lymph nodes were involved, but none were this time. I felt a stronger tie to life, yet this new storm was gaining on me.

Surgery crashed right into my book launch week, planned for May. Medical priorities pushed aside my hopes and dreams, I felt my age as I recovered from surgery. I met with my oncologist, who explained that DNA analysis on the tumor will determine whether I should have chemotherapy. More waiting. DNA results indicated that chemotherapy was not needed, and everyone was pleased, including all the family members whom we'd been regularly updating. I was relieved.

A month after surgery, my sister, who is terrified of flying and never gets on a plane alone, flew solo to spend ten days with me. Together we participated in two in-person book events, talking about our childhood, and my heart hummed with happiness.

Radiation was scheduled for late July. On five consecutive days of treatment, I lay on the radiation table with my hands over my head grasping bars, and held my breath for each dose. I felt exposed and vulnerable and weepy, even though the time required was short.

The storm kept blowing. I expected to have a quick recovery, but exhaustion set in.

The weeks ticked on, and slowly I regained energy, but my balance was off, and I strained a muscle in my back. More medical appointments. Online, I focused on momentum for my book while my blog lay fallow. I restarted occasional walks in my community at a slower pace. My husband was by my side until he was sure I was steady and strong enough to restart my habit of walking alone, listening to podcasts. Raging tinnitus came and went. I started an estrogen blocker, trusting the tiny pill to keep my CHEK2 mutation at bay.

I received cards from friends who are cancer survivors. Readers posted deeply touching reviews about my book. I remembered my sister's visit with joy and messaged her often. Special friends sent me silly animal videos that made me laugh. Optimism resurfaced as I learned to be gentler with my expectations for recovery. The storm morphed into a breeze of restoration. I feel a new kinship with a statement by artist Ted DeGrazia: 'All my paintings are completed but never finished.'"

Angela L. Hoy, Washington State, USA.

Catriona

"Why did it take me so long to understand that you can't control life, or people? Six decades—one might think that I would have learned more in that time."

Louise

"You can't plan life. When you try to plan life you are simply trying to control life. I learned this the hard way. I made grand plans for myself and my family, and none of them turned out the way I planned. Instead, I experienced disappointment—because of my preconceived ideas of how things should be—but also, once I let go of wanting to control everything, immense joy and in unexpected ways. We can't just move through life like we are filling out a checklist, we need a more fluid approach. It is only then that life unfolds, and often in beautiful ways. You just have to give life—and yourself—a chance."

Chapter Twenty-Two

Rebecca

Discovering self

While some long for retirement, with carefully made plans to execute, others struggle with the idea of a future that does not involve work.

"In my long career, almost fifty years of working, I've exceeded my own expectations but it has taken decades for me to become comfortable with success. At least, that is how people described me, as successful. For my part, the more accomplished I became, a scrapbook of articles and many accolades, the more I wanted to do, so the perceived success was always elusive to me, as is the final result, the day I retire. What then?

And what is success, anyway? Yes, I've traveled extensively, and I have the satisfaction of owning property, which allows me to buy what I want without worrying. I've been able to financially support my parents in their later years, until they died, and I've helped a niece and a nephew attend college by setting up funds for them. I give regularly to causes that interest me.

I started a business back in my twenties, and I was fortunate enough to secure, over time, the proper support and backing to grow that business into a multinational brand. However, I believe my real talent, aside from the initial idea behind the company, which I view as accidental more than anything else, is in identifying and hiring the right people. That alone is the skill of which I am most proud. I am a good listener, and I am motivated to help people perform at their best in the working environment they find themselves in.

Other than a few miscalculations, where I haven't followed my instinct about hiring people, I have a loyal staff of whom I am very proud. My role at the company involves focusing on the people culture, and I entrust staff to help others manage various aspects of the business, such as the supply chain, with my input, of course.

But what next? I am seventy-two, and while I am in generally good health, I am slowing down. I never married, and I do not have a partner to share the rest of my life with. Most of my relationships were with men who found it difficult, if I'm honest, to handle my success. I overcompensated to the extent that I was no longer myself, and therefore, I was miserable in our relationships, trying to hide my achievements. I had one relationship with a man who also owned and operated his own business and it felt as if there were four people in the relationship—two humans and two companies; it made for a very crowded bed. We argued a great deal over small things in attempts to avoid the larger issues that were contributing to the ultimate breakdown of the relationship.

I keep working, mostly because I don't know what else to do. I have considered semi-retirement, but I am doubtful if this would suit my personality, as I prefer to be fully immersed in whatever I am doing. It's my company; I still hold the majority of shares, and at this point, I get to choose when I retire. However, settling on a specific retirement date is a challenge.

Retiring doesn't mean selling the business, but I am not sure I could retire and watch other people run my company, probably in a way that I may not like. My friends suggest organizations and groups I could volunteer with, and colleagues have mentioned boards on which I could sit. While this all sounds interesting, my difficulty is picturing a life when I don't get up and go to work to be with the people I have chosen to run my business. Other people's businesses and boards might sound interesting, but sharing my knowledge comes with the risk of the loss I anticipate feeling once my company is sold.

I realize that I have a lot of life yet to live, but I don't know how to live it. That's my problem. I've only known how to live my life in one direction, one way. I sense that it may take the rest of the decade of my seventies to explore what I want to do, and that's not such a bad thing if I allow myself to enjoy the process. It's been a great life so far, and if I remain open and active, and positive, who knows what this decade will bring, but it is my decade and one that I am grateful to experience and to be able to shape."

Maryanne

"I have to admit that I find myself exasperated by all the negativity around women and aging, yet I have mixed feelings, if I am honest, about responses. Defiant, bare-it-all comments seem to push 'aging women' into everyone's face. I don't feel that way. Why, suddenly, in our sixties and seventies, do we need an 'accept us—warts and all—approach?'

At the same time, I realize that we really are the first generations to attempt changing the narrative around older women. My grandmother and mother were not viewed in the same way that I am today. They were just 'old.' And largely forgotten. So, I think extremes are necessary if the message is to be heard by all."

Chapter Twenty-Three

Lucy

Crafting a new life

Downsizing takes on a different dimension when a tiny house is involved. A city dweller, Lucy took a deep breath and faced her future in a small space, surrounded by a semi-rural environment.

"Interior design and decoration have always been of interest to me. When I was married, my husband and I moved around, and I had the opportunity to decorate several homes in different parts of the country. I loved it: repurposing the furniture we already had and adding new pieces, choosing paint colors, and trying out many of the ideas I had seen in magazines and online.

My husband was happy with the end result, but I always wanted more, so when he was given a job in another city or state, I was happy to move again. We moved every three years. That's a lot of homes over thirty years. We didn't own all of them. Some we rented because we were uncertain about how long we would stay, or the property market didn't seem viable at the time for investment.

After I got divorced, I downsized into an apartment and sold most of my larger furniture. It did not seem that there were any more moves in my future—or so I thought. My ex-husband continued to travel for his work and eventually settled in another state. After decades of moving around, I had stopped moving, settled in one place, and it felt odd.

It took me a while to adjust to the limitations of decorating an apartment, just two bedrooms, and once I had completed the project, I became really restless.

I looked for a job and found one—I was still in my late fifties at this point, and landed a job at an interior design store. While this seemed like a good idea at the time, it was not a good idea because I wanted to take home many of the things in the store, and I spent far too much money, even with my employee discount, on furniture and accessories, pillows, vases, rugs and anything else that caught my eye.

I worked for ten years in this job, helping people design and decorate their homes while selling the furniture in the store. Several times, I accompanied the store owners to the biannual markets where, of course, being acquisitive, I saw more things I wanted for my own home.

It didn't take long before I found myself with just too much 'stuff,' and although we like to think others might want our things—because we love them—selling furniture and accessories wasn't easy or profitable at all. I would say that I sold everything at a loss.

It was around my seventieth birthday when I received a letter that changed my life. During the divorce we had separated out our finances equally, including the proceeds from the sale of the house we were living in at the time, as well as our savings. I'd bought an apartment, and even though I had a job, albeit one that I was finding increasingly difficult to do standing on my feet all day, I'd spent a lot of money over the years and now found that I had very little left to live on.

The letter was a herald, announcing that I would run out of money in less than ten years at my current rate of living and spending. Around that time, the owners of the interior design store, who were also around my age, informed me that they had sold the business and that the new owners would no longer need me.

Drastic action was needed. There were several weeks when I was alternately cold and hot with panic. My brother was helpful and he made practical suggestions, most of which I didn't like at first, but I soon realized I would have to sell my apartment and find something smaller to reduce my expenses.

I looked. I searched further and further afield, away from the town I was living in. I felt that I couldn't tell my friends, but at some point I would need to come up with an explanation. My property explorations were taken alone. There was no one to discuss the pros and cons of different places; my brother wasn't interested in evaluating the houses with me.

Most of the places I viewed were very disappointing. Like so many of us, I have mixed feelings about our online world, but there is no doubt that the information provided can be helpful. I stumbled (or did I?) onto articles about tiny homes. At first, I thought they were *far too small for me,* but the more I looked, the more I realized that a tiny home presented a viable option for me—if, and this was a big if, I was willing to reshape and rescale my life.

Perhaps I didn't have an option.

After three months of research, I found a tiny home in a community located about twenty-five miles from where I lived. Most of my concerns were addressed. The tiny home community was located in an older RV park that had been substantially improved, including upgrades such as a vegetable garden and a designated dog park. There were homes to rent or buy, and I was pleasantly surprised by the different layouts. The people seemed friendly and respected each other's privacy.

Another review of my finances, and I realized I shouldn't wait much longer. Fortunately, my apartment sold quickly, and with the cash released, I bought a tiny home. The buyers of my apartment, a couple, liked my things and bought many items from me, which was a great relief because everything needed to be resized: sofas, lamps, beds—even accessories—wouldn't fit into my new home.

I would no longer need night-stands or occasional tables, sofa tables or consoles, or a large coffee table. Almost everything would need to be built-in to create as much floor space as possible. I had far too many lamps, standing lamps, desk lamps, and table lamps.

My experience with interior decoration kicked in, and I began a serious study of space saving. Although I wasn't one hundred percent sold on the idea of living in a tiny home, I realized that I could make it work and began to enjoy the process of decorating on a small scale.

I bought a single-level-home, being smart, for once, about the future. I am getting too old to climb into a loft to go to sleep, or climb down a ladder to go to the bathroom in the middle of the night.

The owners of the tiny home community ask me regularly if they can show my home to potential buyers as an example of what can be done with a tiny home. They are considering setting up a showhouse that I would decorate, and I am having business cards printed so that people can hire me to help them. I've found someone to give me pointers on setting up a social media presence. At this point, I'm unsure that it's needed, but I must say I enjoy all the 'likes' when my photographs are admired by others.

Yes, it's been an adjustment, but I feel more in control of my life. I will be the first person to say that things haven't turned out the way I expected, and I know I'm not alone in this. Whatever adaptations and adjustments I thought were necessary in my sixties were just the beginning. We can't expect to sail through our seventies to calm waters, as much as we might want to. Health becomes the most significant preoccupation—both physical and mental—but I have found community here, with other owners of tiny homes, in the last place I expected it. Life is good if you are open to navigating the twists and turns."

she's gone to great lengths to be liked—that in itself is a big mistake in my view—are challenging for her, so I cannot imagine how lonely she is.

My friend spends most of her time managing the things that she perceives are important to her husband—or maybe feeding a need in herself to be liked and needed? I have often wondered what would happen if she just stopped trying to please everybody.

She assures me that she has a nice life, living comfortably financially and able to pursue hobbies; the reality is that this life is economically and emotionally attached to the man she married.

The concept of being alone—for my friend in her seventies—is not something that I believe she could allow herself to contemplate, although statistically, her husband will die before her and she will be alone. When I bring this up, she talks about a rosy future where she and her husband will be together—in what retirement home, I want to ask? I am more of a realist, but I understand she is a dreamer.

I can't decide whether she lost herself or found herself. Or maybe she never changed, and I was the one who didn't recognize her because my version of my best friend is rooted in the past and not today.

To me, she is not the vibrant person I met in college—full of ideas—or the woman I knew in her twenties, thirties, forties, fifties or even sixties. She was there for me

Chapter Twenty-Four

Gloria Stone

Resilience creates opportunity for reinvention

After burying her immediate family—husband, son, and daughter—Gloria moved to Mexico. She says she doesn't know if she is living or running, but she is determined not to drown in an abyss of grief. At eighty-three she is doing what she pleases, on her own terms and in her own time, and encouraging others through her social media presence to do the same thing.

"As a product of the hippy era—the sixties and seventies—I had battled drug, alcohol, and cocaine addition while raising my son and daughter. In 1982, I saw three roads ahead of me; either live sober, die, or kill someone while driving drunk. I chose to become clean and sober, kicking a heavy drug habit and alcohol dependency, finally releasing myself from the tentacles of both.

But my husband was also an addict and never stopped using even while he was sick, so it wasn't until I had nursed him through bone cancer and dying, ten years later in

1992, that I felt the psychological prison door open, and I was free.

Phone calls change your life. When I was sixty-six years old, in 2007, I heard that my son was gravely ill with amyotrophic lateral sclerosis (ALS) and dying. He died two years later, and at that time, I fought for and gained custody of his son, my grandson, Dylan, who was seven years old.

The day your child dies alters you forever; the subsequent grief is experienced as a dark, sad, and lonely journey for which there is no help. And I was alone; my husband had died, and I was dealing with the terrible grief of losing a child while trying to raise another child, one who was in first grade. As I saw it, I had no choice but to resolve to 'get up, get strong, and go on.' It took me four long years before I ventured back out of the fog to a very different life.

I raised my grandson, did all the things expected of a parent—and grandparent—in that position, and Dylan is now twenty-five years old, thriving, loving, and happy.

It was my turn, and I began living what I thought of as a good life, working and traveling with my little dog. I'd bought a nice RV, lived through COVID-19, and life was easy again: I was living a kind of peace that I hadn't known before, until once more my world completely turned upside down.

In 2022, I received news that my daughter had been diagnosed with colon cancer. We stayed in touch with Face-

Time, but in December 2023, I received another phone call. This time, the call was from my granddaughter to say that her mother, my daughter, had died—no trauma, no injuries, no hospital stay, just peacefully going to sleep one night before joining her father and brother.

The woman that I had been for eighty-one years, quietly, and silently, died at that moment. I felt shocked, broken, alone, and utterly devastated. I went into seclusion, thinking, *How do I survive this, and will I?*

Something told me that I had to leave, to get away, to change my life or be consumed by grief. I searched for and found a pet-sitting situation in Cerritos Beach, Mexico, and packed a duffle bag before boarding a plane to Mexico. I was eighty-two years old.

In January of 2025, I returned to the US, sold everything I owned, and moved permanently to Zihuatanejo, Mexico. My life now is about sharing. I am on a mission to share my story in order to give hope to others. I feel that my followers on social media want to hear from me, about my travels, my grief, my hopes, and inspirations. My message is, 'Live life, do not just exist.'"

Gloria Stone, Zihuatanejo, Mexico.

Pauline

"As so many women have done before us, we must show our daughters and granddaughters the way forward, by our example. They live in the present, not our past. Their values are different and we need to recognize that. It is up to us to adapt, not for younger generations to help us turn the world back into something we recognize. It is our job to remain current, and forward thinking, or, at the very least, not complain about a time that exists only in our minds.

If we show our daughters and granddaughters the possibilities and opportunities that are available for us in our seventies, by our actions, by living vibrant lives, we are providing them with a roadmap. We won't be around to see it, but we should take heart that we did our job to encourage them to pursue their dreams."

Chapter Twenty-Five

Marjorie

Making peace with life while discovering new joy

Finally, a decade that presents Marjorie with more free time and the courage to indulge in her own creativity—regardless of what anyone else thinks.

"People say that in our sixties and seventies, we are free to explore our creativity—let's assuming we possess creativity! My creativity is quiet. I don't talk about it. I take photographs with my cell phone, print them, cut them, and paste the images into a collage. I suppose it's creative. It gives me pleasure, anyway.

I have endless scrapbooks on different subjects. It feels like a schoolgirl hobby to me, but I like it nonetheless. When I am working on these projects, I experience a sense of calm, of peace, almost a trancelike state, and a sense of completeness.

I photograph only small things: insects, small flowers and leaves, sometimes twigs. I select only objects that I see on a small scale, even a small section of a small thing—the tinier the better, as if I like to reduce my world to something miniature and insignificant but still part of our big world. The scale appeals to me. Perhaps it has something to do with my response to the massive scale of life today, of things rushing by, of the often-incomprehensible world we live in.

I do not have a plan. It is not my intention to share my scrapbooks or sell my works. The truth is I'm not even really sure if my art—or is it craft?—is any good. And whereas I once cared about this, I am no longer bothered.

It's taken me a while to get to this point, when I wake up everyday, relatively free of duties and obligations, and think about what I might photograph today. There is an intense feeling of pleasure, one I keep to myself. It's mine alone unlike everything else in my life, which I share with my husband.

Like many couples in our sixties, my husband and I downsized our home, moving out of the four-bedroom house we'd lived in for over twenty years.

Our children had settled in different states and were busy getting on with their lives. We reached a point where we felt the house was too large for us and wanted a different lifestyle, although we couldn't have described exactly what that would be; we wanted life on a smaller scale. The search began for a smaller property.

For months, we had a back-and-forth conversation with our children about moving to 'somewhere remote,' as they viewed our selections of towns, but we finally decided to move to a coastal village in the north of the country. Our thought process was that the children might continue to move to different states before settling, and we were not in a position to follow them. Instead, we would put down our anchor somewhere, and then the children would have to come and visit us.

My husband and I sold off lots of our furniture, the children didn't want any of it, declaring it to be 'too brown' and 'not modern enough for our style.' Unlike earlier generations when people were grateful for inherited furniture! We found a much smaller home with a garage and a workshop. My husband has a passion for woodworking, so he was very excited about the prospect of spending a large part of his day in a new space where he could tinker all day.

Now I don't see him from after breakfast until dinner, unless we happen to run into each other around lunchtime, in the kitchen, when we each make our favorite sandwiches. If we want to avoid conversation, we alter our lunch hour.

Once we'd moved into our new home, with all the upheaval associated with downsizing and adjusting to a new town, we finally began to settle in. While we missed some of the things we'd given away, we soon learned to adapt. If you have less, I think you need less.

I joined local groups in the hope of finding a social life for us. As there were so many people of a similar age to us in the small town, it didn't take long. Our neighbors were friendly and very hospitable, and soon we had a social life, in and out of each other's houses, celebrating birthdays, anniversaries, and events. We feel fortunate because, after hearing the experiences of other friends, we realize that small communities are not always welcoming to new people, particularly single people.

I found women I could walk with regularly, and I volunteered for several local organizations they recommended. Of course, it's difficult to make friends later in life, so I tend to think of these friends as new acquaintances, as yet-to-be friends. But the truth is that as we age, we need people, people to socialize with, people to help in emergencies when family is far away.

And then in my spare time, of which there is plenty these days, I picked up my old hobby again, only this time, given our proximity to the beach and water, I could photograph grains of sand, grass, the occasional seashell, and anything else I found on my walks by the seashore. There are different plants, rocks, and stones, as well as leaves, flowers, and branches. My days are full of discovery as I explore the new part of the world I live in.

Sometimes, I feel that I am living two lives. With my husband, I am unchanged. I organize, prepare, and schedule everything. I love it when we have the chance to spend time together with our children, an event which I also help organize. I am skilled at managing a household, preparing meals, and cultivating a social life. My husband helps, but we have defined roles and a traditional marriage. He can be outgoing and friendly, but we are old companions now, old friends. I don't really have any other expectations, not after forty years of marriage.

On occasion, I find myself wistful, for a different life, and if I am honest, for a different man, possibly an imaginary man, one who might be more interested in my hobbies. It's not as if I feel taken for granted, for I have laid out the framework of our marriage carefully, with great forethought, and it functions as it should, at least as I how thought it should when I got married years ago. My mother was a significant influence on me and to some extent, I modeled my marriage after my parents', which, by all accounts, was a successful one.

And then there's my other interior life, a delicious sense of exploration, discovery, and creativity.

I've had a good life—I'm still having one. I'd like to see more of my adult children, but perhaps that will happen in time, as they get older, marry, and have children of their own and want to include the grandparents.

Life—and marriage—is a compromise. That's nothing new. Nods acknowledge this, shrugs, and side glances in a room full of older married couples, all of us sitting together in various states of fitness—mental and physical—when we discuss our mutual interests and lifestyle choices and we avoid the topic of long-term compatibility when, over time, our interests inevitably change.

In our mid and late sixties and early seventies, we each made our compromises, individually and as couples, and and while most of us have come to terms with the contracts we executed years ago, and most of us—not all—have signed up for a life of these contract negotiations, softened and molded over the years, we might still wish for more.

But I am content. I have my 'hobby,' and for now, that will sustain me through many things."

———※———

Chapter Twenty-Six

Epilogue - last words

If one hasn't realized that life is short, the seventies heavily underline this awareness.

In my mid-sixties, I took up gardening, or urban dirt digging as I call it, as this seems to be a more accurate description. I found endless sources of inspiration and education online, although I admit in my eagerness to see results, I became an experimental gardener: one who reads the instructions after the fact and therefore learns by a longer, more painstaking method.

Gardening, like life, is about successes and failures, about trial and error, about joyous results and disappointments we'd rather not share or perhaps even admit to. There is the weather to contend with, weather patterns that hold the same unpredictability that we find in life. When we expect the sun, there are showers. The wind blows through and disrupts many of our well-laid plans, while devastating droughts and storms occur, and all of a sudden, unpredictable sunshine appears.

But more than anything, tending a garden, even a balcony garden, reminds us of the passing of time. With gardening, there is always a next year to repeat the successes. "I'll conserve these seeds to sow next year," or in the spring, "I'll turn over this bed and plant again." There will be another spring, summer, fall, and winter. Another chance to repeat what was successful and to try again to succeed where we failed before. Always a future to plan for, and one we take for granted. Just like life.

How many more seasons will we see? As the writers have pointed out, in our seventies we are all getting closer to mortality. And the perennial plants, just like the people and the other things in our life, will continue without us when we are gone.

When you think about it this way why would anyone spend any more time on a sofa than absolutely necessary? If one is curious about anything in life, now is the time to explore while we still can. It is also a time to catch up on old hobbies and interests, setting aside the pressures of daily life, which may have involved raising a family, attending to caretaking responsibilities, and working.

In my case, I have long held onto a closet full of textiles, many of which are old, and just as many are very beautiful and challenging to find these days, with only a vague idea of what to do with them.

Growing up, we recall that there were, for the most part, two ways of dressing: one for special occasions and one for everyday. Fashion then had far more rules than it does today.

There was a greater distinction between day clothes and evening clothes—especially if you were not a teenager or someone in their twenties. And there were distinctions between work clothes, formal clothes, and evening clothes. The athletic clothing that is everywhere today, sweatshirts, T-shirts, leggings, jogging pants, hoodies, and anoraks—in various colors and soft, rounded shapes—was unthinkable thirty or forty years ago.

So what, I asked myself, *do I do with my fabrics and vintage jewelry—particularly brooches; how many people do you see wearing brooches these days?—and the other items I have collected over the years?* It's rare today to see women wearing a lot of jewelry, and if I am honest, lots of jewelry just looks dated.

If I am true to myself, I will cut up these fabrics and stitch—or have them made—into the clothes I want to wear. And I will wear my costume jewelry, because what am I waiting for? I am far beyond seeking anyone's approval. So the woman you see at the grocery store, in a brilliant taffeta skirt and an unusual brooch, that might be me, living my best life.

On a more serious note, I am interested how fashion has developed due to embargoes imposed by different countries on one another. A shortage of one textile may have resulted in an explosive trend of another textile in a fashion history twist on supply and demand. But, I expect this is a book that might only interest me, and even if that's the case, there's nothing to prevent me from writing it—except myself!

I plan to write short stories and fiction, which is an entirely new venture for me and one I am settling into and becoming quite comfortable with. It's fun to explore new territories, to stretch and learn, and at this point I can't see a time when I will stop living, loving, enjoying being around people of all ages and backgrounds, and special times with family. There's no need to ask for more, because depending on how we frame our lives, we have what we need, and what we don't have may not have been meant for us.

Chapter Twenty-Seven

More about the essayists

Linda Cahan
https://www.lindacahan.com/

Nancy Cahan
https://nancycahan.weebly.com/

Lucia Cavalcanti de Albuquerque
https://luciacavalcanti.com/

Angela L. Hoy
Children Born of Wildfire: A Memoir
https://www.angelahoywriter.com/

Chapter Twenty-Eight

About the author

Georgina O'Hara Callan's early career began in London, UK, as a journalist for women's magazines, a ghostwriter, and a magazine editor. Her first book was about financial advice for women, written at a time when many women did not have full control over their own money.

For her second book, she spent a year in Paris, France, researching the history of fashion and fashion design from the early 1800s, when the invention of the home sewing machine became a functional and creative tool for many women, simultaneously changing fashion forever. Research for this book required extensive travel to the USA and within the UK and Europe. *The Thames & Hudson Dictionary of Fashion and Fashion Designers* was translated into multiple languages, and *Vogue* labeled the book a "fashion bible."

After moving to the USA in 1985, Georgina published two more books: one on infancy and the culture of nurture throughout the centuries, and the other on the social history of marriage, examining how the original business and contractual arrangement of marriage has evolved.

Georgina lived for twenty years in New Orleans, Louisiana, and after Hurricane Katrina (2005), moved to Dallas, Texas, where she continued to raise her sons, who are now grown with families of their own.

After several decades, when she paused writing to raise a family and start a design and textiles business, causing her to travel extensively both nationally and internationally, Georgina returned to writing, initially by interviewing architects, designers, and creatives for various publications. She describes her life as being "book-ended." She started writing in her twenties and now, in her late sixties—almost seventy—and after a life full of experiences and many tales to tell, she is writing once again. In mid-2025 she published *Sixty and Speaking Up,* her sixth book. *Seventy and Speaking Up* is her seventh book.